DEVELOPING SERVANT
LEADERS AT SCALE

The first move I made after launching the New Politics Leadership Academy was to hire Max. Nobody else knew how to do this kind of deep inner work at scale. Thanks to the approach shared in this book, the thousands of servant leaders who have come through our programs are more connected to their own "why", more conscious of their own shadow, and more able to lead with clarity and integrity. And now hundreds are elected leaders at every level from School Board to Congress. Max's approach is proven, tested, powerful, and vitally important at this critical moment for democracy here in the United States and around the world.

—*Emily Cherniack*, **Founder and Executive Director of New Politics and the New Politics Leadership Academy, named to the Politico 50, a list of "thinkers, dreamers, and doers driving politics" in 2018**

In a world brimming with complex challenges, *Developing Servant Leaders at Scale* is not just a book; it's a roadmap to a better, brighter future.

—*Laura Gassner Otting*, **ABC Contributor and *Wall Street Journal* Bestselling Author of *Wonderhell***

Max Klau's latest book gives you the tools to cultivate leadership that's both transformational and deeply human. He challenges leaders to reflect on their core values and step boldly into the courage required to lead with authenticity. This book isn't just about building better organizations – it's about building better people. If you're serious about scaling servant leadership and fostering inner growth in yourself and others, this is the guide you've been waiting for.

—*Lt. Colonel Amy McGrath*, **US Marine Corps (ret.), a political and national security expert, a former fighter pilot and founder of Democratic Majority Action PAC, and former Democratic nominee for the US House and Senate from Kentucky**

In a time when our nation is hungry for purpose-driven leadership, *Developing Servant Leaders at Scale* offers a roadmap for the kind of transformation we so desperately need. As a combat veteran, an entrepreneur, and now a member of Congress, I've learned that real leadership isn't about titles or ego—it's about service. And as Max Klau makes clear, true servant leadership begins within. It challenges us to connect with our deepest sense of purpose and confront our own shadow—the fears, biases, and blind spots that limit our ability to lead with authenticity. That inner work isn't optional; it's essential. This book does more than just make the case for servant leadership—it's a how-to guide that presents a proven, tested approach to developing servant leaders at scale. You can take my word for it: This stuff works.

—*Congressman Pat Ryan*, **US Representative, NY-18; former Army officer and tech entrepreneur**

Klau tunnels through a mountain of literature with a path to inspiring servant leadership at a scale sufficient to address complex 21st century challenges. This is a book to meet our moment, both deeply personal and widely applicable for anyone who wishes to deliver transformational experiences at scale.

—*Julia Fabris McBride*, **Chief Learning and Development Officer, Kansas Leadership Center**

Max Klau's groundbreaking work illuminates a profound truth: a leader's inner development and outer impact are inextricably linked. Through decades of rigorous experimentation and practice, he has created a sophisticated yet practical framework for developing servant leaders at scale. His Flame model elegantly integrates personal growth with organizational leadership effectiveness, while his Journey approach provides a tested methodology for guiding transformational inner work in professional settings. The parallel emergence of Klau's experientially derived framework and the more recent UN Inner Development Goals (IDGs) reveals a powerful convergence in leadership thinking. At a moment when our world desperately needs purpose-driven leaders, Klau offers hard-won wisdom about how organizations can systematically develop people who lead from a deep sense of calling rather than ego.

—*Steve Boyd*, Founder,
Washington Governors' School for Citizen
Leadership; Principal, MacDonald Boyd
and Associates, Seattle

Max Klau's book transcends traditional leadership literature by offering a deeply practical blueprint for building leadership development systems at scale. Drawing from his rich experiences at two major servant-leader organizations, Max demonstrates that effective leadership in today's challenging world requires both external action and internal transformation. Through vulnerable self-reflection, he reveals how, individually and collectively, confronting our "shadow" – the unconscious forces driving our behavior – is essential for authentic leadership. The Flame model he presents makes a compelling case that scaling leadership development demands more than just skills and knowledge; it requires transformative experiences that foster spiritual growth. This book is a masterful blend of personal narrative and actionable insights for anyone committed to developing leaders at scale.

—*Hugh O'Doherty*, **Founding member, the Leadership and Peacemaking Global Network**

This book is a game-changer for those who want to enter the arena of public service. Max's approach to servant leadership is not only simple but profoundly powerful – and was instrumental as I prepped for my mayoral campaign. I wholeheartedly endorse this book for anyone who wants to make a lasting difference in the world.

—*Philip Jones*, **Mayor of Newport News, Virginia & Marine Corps Vet**

Max Klau is wise. His wisdom is honed from his being, knowing, and doing the hard work of servant leadership development shared through his insightful stories of those experiences in compelling situations. Klau has been there and earns the trust of readers with his refreshing candor and reflection. This book is perfect for readers who seek to empower their organizations toward more purposeful action on their shared missions.

—*Susan R. Komives* **is a Professor Emerita from the University of Maryland. Her books include Exploring Leadership and Leadership for a Better World. She is a recipient of the Lifetime Achievement Award from the International Leadership Association**

In Developing Servant Leaders, Max Klau presents an actionable and timely guide for cultivating leaders driven by service, compassion, and a commitment to the common good. He generously shares hard-won and well-researched insights on what does and doesn't work when fostering inner development in leaders everywhere. I couldn't put it down once I started because it contained so many helpful insights.

—Chalon Bridges, **Chief Experience Officer, The Flight School.org**

Developing Servant Leaders at Scale is precisely the resource needed at a time when the most prominent examples of leadership are ego-centric and autocratic. Max shares a journey of inquiry, experience, and continual learning, which produced a model of leadership development and behavior that is transforming individuals and organizations. His quest exemplifies the power and practice of self-knowledge and reflection and has given us a framework and process with the potential to change us and the world for all people.

—Katherine Tyler-Scott, **Leadership consultant, coach, author, and speaker. She is the co-founder and Managing Principal of KI Thoughtbridge, LLC, and past President of the International Leadership Association**

Imagine a world where leaders at every level of society are driven to serve others and create lasting positive change for their communities. This is the future that Dr. Max Klau shows us how to build through his groundbreaking approach to developing servant leaders at scale. Drawing on decades of experience training thousands of social entrepreneurs and aspiring public servants, Dr. Klau's integrated frameworks provide organizational leaders and philanthropists with essential tools for cultivating leaders whose inner clarity enables them to create better futures for those they hope to serve.

—Patrick Dowd, **Entrepreneur and Board President, The Long Now Foundation**

For anyone who aspires to be a servant leader and to create a powerful organizational capacity for change, *Developing Servant Leaders at Scale* illuminates the need and holds the key. Max Klau, through describing his life's work, explains the urgent need of today's leaders to understand the connection between inner and outer change and why it matters at this critical moment.

—*Cynthia Cherrey*, **President,**
International Leadership Association

Max Klau's book, *Developing Servant Leaders at Scale*, is a comprehensive "Tour De Force" regarding both the conceptual underpinnings and the practical how-to of developing leaders dedicated to the common good. I was privileged to work alongside of and learn from Dr. Klau at City Year for more than a decade as he developed the "Idealist Journey" curriculum. I witnessed the care and evolution of the process. He skillfully guided a cadre of young leaders across the nation capable of navigating a transformative experience in making meaning of a year of community service in our nation's schools and communities. Dr. Klau makes a compelling case for why this work is vital to the future of our society. This book captures the essence, magic and impact as well as the pragmatic steps needed to create a new generation of servant leaders which are so desperately needed as we confront the challenges before us.

—*Charlie Rose*, **Senior Vice President and**
Dean, City Year

In this thoughtful book, Max Klau skillfully demonstrates how servant leaders might better connect inner and outer change processes in support of flourishing for themselves and those they serve. What sets this book apart is the roadmap it provides to help organizations do this at scale. I especially appreciated Max's candor about the difficult learning journey that he and colleagues at City Year had to take to iterate a set of reflective and service practices that actually worked for large groups, including initial critics, and not just for a subset of motivated self-selectors. Unlike other books in this genre, this narrative hinges on leadership as a collective capacity, as well as Max's specific contributions. I hope that it finds a wide audience!

—*Matthew T. Lee*, **Director of the Flourishing Network at the Human Flourishing Program at Harvard University, Scientific Advisor to the Inner Development Goals Foundation, Professor at Baylor University**

We are living in an age that desperately needs to develop more (and more!) servant leaders. No one is better positioned than Max Klau to know what's required to take on this daunting but essential task. In this book, Klau blends fascinating personal stories with deep expertise with well-researched theories with practical tools to offer just the roadmap that our organizations, communities, and society need now more than ever. If a central task of leadership is to develop more leaders, this book is required reading for every leader whose impact and legacy matters to them.

—*Jeff Wetzler*, **Co-Founder of Transcend and Author of** *Ask: Tap Into the Hidden Wisdom of People Around You for Unexpected Breakthroughs in Leadership and Life*

In a world torn by division and crisis, how do we cultivate leaders who truly serve? This groundbreaking book reveals how to develop servant leaders at scale – expanding leadership beyond individual efforts to create systemic change. Drawing on decades of experience, Max Klau maps a must-read blue-print for leaders who prioritize improving the lives of others.

—*Betsy Myers*, **Chief Operating Officer for Obama's 2008 national campaign; Founding director of the Center for Women and Business at Bentley University and former Executive Director of the Center for Public Leadership Harvard's Kennedy School; Author of** *Take the Lead: Motivate, Inspire and Bring Out the Best in Yourself and Everyone Around You*

In a world increasingly dominated by self-serving leaders who prioritize power over purpose, Max Klau's *Developing Servant Leaders at Scale* arrives as an urgently needed blueprint for cultivating the kind of leadership our troubled times demand. Drawing from decades of experience building leadership capacity at organizations like City Year and New Politics Leadership Academy, Klau presents a sophisticated yet practical framework for developing leaders who put service above self. His "Flame and Journey" model, refined through years of real-world application, offers organizations a proven approach to nurturing the inner development and outer skills required for authentic servant leadership. This book is essential reading for anyone committed to developing leaders who can help heal our divided world through the transformative power of serving others first.

—*Ejaj Ahmad*, **Founder, Bangladesh Youth Leadership Center & Global Youth Leadership Center**

Developing Servant Leaders at Scale recognizes a profoundly important, but often overlooked foundation for getting things done and for creating a more just world: As you address local, national, and international challenges, make sure to invest in and nurture the potential of the people who are working hard to make a difference. This book draws upon years of hands-on work on the ground and the wisdom Klau brings us thanks to his sharp, thoughtful mind, always eager to learn from the people with whom he works. This is a book that will help you make a difference and will make a difference in you.

—*Dan Rothstein*, Co-founder,
The Right Question Institute

DEVELOPING SERVANT LEADERS AT SCALE

How to Do It, and Why It Matters

BY

MAX KLAU

The Center for Courageous Wholeness, USA

FOREWORD BY

ROSABETH MOSS KANTER

emerald
PUBLISHING

United Kingdom – North America – Japan – India
Malaysia – China

Emerald Publishing Limited
Emerald Publishing, Floor 5, Northspring, 21-23 Wellington Street, Leeds LS1 4DL

First edition 2025

Reprints and permissions service
Contact: www.copyright.com

British Library Cataloguing in Publication Data
A catalogue record for this book is available from the British Library

ISBN: 978-1-83708-165-3 (Print)
ISBN: 978-1-83708-162-2 (Online)
ISBN: 978-1-83708-164-6 (Epub)

INVESTOR IN PEOPLE

For Bev, Bernie, and Sadie.

And in honor of my father, David Klau (z"l), whose life was the embodiment of servant leadership.

QUOTES

The servant-leader *is* servant first... It begins with the natural feeling that one wants to serve, to serve *first*. Then conscious choice brings one to aspire to lead. That person is sharply different from one who is leader first, perhaps because of the need to assuage an unusual power drive or to acquire material possessions.

– Robert K. Greenleaf

For we move—each—in two worlds: The inward of our own awareness and an outwards of participation in the history of our time and place.

– Joseph Campbell

CONTENTS

ABOUT THE AUTHOR

Dr. Max Klau is the Founder of the Center for Courageous Wholeness, an organization dedicated to helping individuals and organizations integrate shadow, serve others, and scale their impact. He recently served as the Chief Program Officer at the New Politics Leadership Academy (NPLA), an organization focused on bringing more servant leaders–military vets and alumni of national service programs like AmeriCorps and Peace Corps–into politics. Prior to that, he was the Vice President of Leadership Development at City Year, the education-focused AmeriCorps program. He received his doctorate from the Harvard Graduate School of Education in 2005 with a focus on human development and leadership.

His second book, *Developing Servant Leaders at Scale: How to Do It and Why It Matters*, will be published in August 2025. He is a husband, a father, a consultant, speaker, an Integral Master Coach, and a musician. He lives outside of Boston with his wife and two children. Learn more about him at http://www.maxklau.com/

FOREWORD

Service, Identity, and Transformational Change
By Rosabeth Moss Kanter

On first blush, I'm an odd choice to write about this book. I'm
a Harvard Business School professor and corporate consultant
focused more on outward than inward change, oriented more
to structures and systems than individual psyches. But I have
long viewed service as a pillar of American democracy and
national service a major force for change, whether that means
doing community work or running for public office. I've had
the privilege to support the service movement (and the mission
Max Klau describes) from inside.

I served for many years on the national Board of Trustees
of City Year, the flagship AmeriCorps program where Klau's
ideas about servant leadership were formed. Later I joined
advisory councils for New Politics, the parent of the leadership academy Klau seeded and grew. In 2005, I co-founded
Harvard University's Advanced Leadership Initiative, which
launched its first cohort in 2009 of top leaders transitioning
from their income-earning years to their next years of service –
and became a model for at least 30 other programs to date
around the world. It was clear that those who rise to the top in
business, government, and NGOs can still learn a thing or two
about leadership that serves others.

Servant leadership is an antidote to selfish, greedy power hoarders who can pepper society with cynicism and let problems fester. My corporate experience made me see the importance of leadership that empowers and lifts others up. That is, empowering, uplifting leadership is important if you want productivity – the ability to meet high performance standards – as well as innovation – the use of imagination to create solutions to perplexing problems. The best corporate CEOs are servant leaders like the ones this book hopes to multiply, operating in the interests of the institution rather than themselves. "Country over self," as New Politics puts it in looking for people who "answer the call."

Service opportunities are themselves a path to leadership development. As Klau explains, City Year was dedicated as much to development for the youthful AmeriCorps members as those young people were trained to foster the growth of the at-risk public school students they served. Indeed, service builds leaders. The iconic technology company IBM created its own service corps for rising executives as a major part of their leadership training. Instead of classrooms, diverse teams worked together to address challenges in many parts of the world.

Max Klau helps point the way to this new model by telling his own story. His book is part memoir, part how-to guidebook. It shows that the journey to create great leaders is as challenging as the journey those leaders face – especially when the trainings are not face to face but at distance and scale.

And Klau helps readers see the connection between outer change and inner change, between organizational purpose and individual passion. Transformational leadership involves looking "outside the building," as I propose it in my recent book, *Think Outside the Building*. But the soul-searching of inner work also helps people see where they are blinded by conventional institutional structures (i.e., "buildings") and helps them find their calling and challenge convention with new ideas.

Inner work at scale, as Klau presents it, flourishes in communities. Flip the pages of the book to see how much people take signals from one another and also pride in their connections. The leadership development techniques he offers support individuals but also important support groups and teams, villages and communities. He came to realize that labels matter because they build shared vocabulary that help people articulate their commonalities as well as differences. He saw the importance of stories, a core City Year leadership principle, especially shared stories told to peers who are willing and informed listeners.

Klau stresses the importance of culture and symbols. A shared culture of service can insulate idealists against the destructive forces of cynicism; it can arm people with courage to persevere when the going is tough. Finding one's inner calling in a group also creates a powerful common identity as change agents. Soon after my colleagues and I created Harvard's Advanced Leadership Initiative, and the first cohort arrived, we were surprised most by the strength of the immediate ties that formed within mere minutes of highly diverse (many countries and professions as well as ethnicities) and highly individualistic people coming together in the name of problem-solving. We think the bonding came in response to a new leadership identity, one better suited to working on big societal problems (such as public education, which Klau highlights) than to getting people in hierarchies to toe the line.

There are many approaches to leadership development; it's a booming industry. But by emphasizing servant leadership and how to engage large numbers of people, Klau adds some new dimensions. He offers a candid personal view of the challenges, and he wrestles with how to do it for many people at once and at a distance. There's more than enough room for everyone who believes in the mission. So let a thousand flowers bloom, and many more. Let empowering tools spread and infuse cultures everywhere with an ethic of service, expressed by leaders who reflect and learn.

Rosabeth Moss Kanter
Arbuckle Professor, Harvard Business School
Founding Chair & Director, Harvard University
Advanced Leadership Initiative (2005-2018)
New book, *Think Outside the Building:*
How Advanced Leaders Can Change the World One
Smart Innovation at a Time

ACKNOWLEDGMENTS

This book essentially tells the story of my life's work, and it's been decades in the making. I can't possibly name every individual who contributed to the growth and evolution of this work over the course of 20 years, but I'm going to do my best to honor the major contributions along the way.

My entire career in leadership was sparked by a class on adaptive leadership taught by Dean Williams at the Kennedy School. I had chances to learn from and with Ron Heifetz and spent multiple semesters as a course assistant for Hugh O'Doherty. They were all master leadership educators, and my life has been shaped in profound ways by my time with them all. Hugh also introduced me to Steve Boyd, who connected me with his daughter Mikaela, who was working at City Year at the time. All the work described in this book grew out of that brief meeting with Mikaela at City Year headquarters in Back Bay.

I'm grateful to the many individuals at City Year who influenced this work and shaped my career at that amazing organization. Gratitude to Michael Brown and Alan Khazei for bringing the idea of City Year to life, and to Dr. Andy Munoz, Stephanie Wu, and Rob Gordon for their leadership. Gratitude to Marc Morgan, Bobby Kessling, Daniel Ready, and literally hundreds of other staff and Senior Corps members who were invaluable partners in making this approach to leadership development powerful and effective. There are far too many to name here, but if you were one of the many City Year staff or AmeriCorps members who played a role in the Idealist's Journey work, thank you for your partnership and contributions. Special thanks are due to Charlie Rose, who was my supervisor for my final several years at City Year. He was an amazing champion for me and this work, and he is one of the most remarkable servant leaders that I have ever met.

Deep gratitude to Dan Rothstein and Luz Santana from the Right Question Institute. As this book makes clear, their work around the Question Formulation Technique was a revelation for me and was a breakthrough in this effort to build an organizational capacity for reflection and inner work. I'm grateful for their wisdom, commitment to democracy, and programmatic brilliance, and hope that this book brings some more much deserved attention and interest to their organization.

Emily Cherniack is a force of nature who saw the potential and value in this work at a time when few others understood its significance. When she invited me to join the New Politics Leadership Academy, it was my belief in her courage, integrity, and leadership that led me to say yes. I'm grateful for the opportunities she gave me and for the chance to learn from and with her during my time at NPLA. I'm grateful to Shaquanda Brown for building from scratch a host of systems and processes to support this work, to Whitney McKnight for more programmatic excellence and being a great thought partner, and to Lucy Arthur-Parately for carrying this work forward so skillfully.

During my time at the New Politics Leadership Academy I had that chance to work with many other amazing colleagues, as well as hundreds of facilitators and program participants. Once again, there are far too many to name individually, but they also played an integral role in the evolution of this work. They are also some of the most inspiring, thoughtful, courageous, and committed servant leaders I've ever met. If you've been an Answering the Call facilitator or have participated in any of the NPLA programming here's my message to you: I appreciate the time, talent, and genius that you dedicated to this work, and knowing that you are out there continuing to serve our nation at this challenging moment gives me faith in our democracy and hope for our future.

Gratitude to Beth Lapin, a distant cousin who replied to my Facebook post asking if anyone had a place I could use for a writing retreat to complete the final draft of this book. I had a very productive few days of writing at her home in New London.

Gratitude to Debra DeRuyer at the International Leadership Association for connecting me with Fiona Allison at Emerald Publishing, and thanks to Fiona for believing in this title. Thanks, also, to Sashikala Balasubramanian, Yemaya Marsden, and the rest of the team at Emerald for their support and partnership in bringing this book out into the world.

This book would not exist without the love and support of my family. My father passed away just a few months before the publication of this book; he was the embodiment of servant leadership, and there are no words to capture the depth of his impact on my life and on my work. My amazing mom is a remarkable servant leader as well, who also continues to model being creative, sharing stories, building community, and treating others with dignity every day.

Thanks to my awesome siblings, Dan, Deb, Michal, and Nate and their equally awesome spouses and kids. Every conversation we've ever had around the family table has shaped this book in a meaningful way.

To my wife, Bev: I couldn't do any of this without you. Thank you for reading every draft multiple times, sharing your thoughts, pushing my thinking, and supporting me when I disappeared for days on writing retreats. Thanks for being my rock during the ups and downs that unfolded as I tried to get this book out into the world. Thanks for filling our home with so much joy and love.

To my kids, Bernie and Sadie: My love for you both is infinite. It is my deepest prayer that these ideas serve humanity as we navigate this time of peril and change in the years ahead.

INTRODUCTION

> *The ultimate aim of the quest must be neither release*
> *nor ecstasy for oneself, but the wisdom and the power*
> *to serve others.* – Joseph Campbell (1988, p. xiv)

We are living through a critical moment in human history. Surrounded by both crisis and opportunity and swept up in the currents of change that move faster and faster each year, we find ourselves confronting multiple overlapping crises unfolding simultaneously. As individuals, communities, organizations, nations, and as a global community, we find ourselves struggling to respond effectively to the moment. We are confronted with the need to find productive ways forward at this time of relentless change and uncertainty.

Amid all this complexity, however, one thing is crystal clear: If we are going to find a productive and positive way through this moment of change and uncertainty, we need more leaders. Not just any kind of leaders, though. All around us we see leaders who crave power and the ability to dominate others, who are driven by selfishness and greed, who use hate and scorn to divide and diminish others, and who seek positions of authority to satisfy personal hungers for significance or love. These are not the leaders we need.

The kind of leaders we need to see a whole lot more of in the years ahead are *servant leaders*. These are individuals who feel a calling to use their gifts and abilities to lift up others.

Whatever power they have, they use to help others become more capable and more free. When they seek positions of greater power or authority, they do so because those positions expand their capacity to serve others. We need to see a lot more of those leaders in the years ahead.

This is a book about how we can develop more of those servant leaders. A lot more.

As the title makes clear, this book pulls together two key ideas: *Servant leadership* and *at scale*.

Servant leadership is both an ancient concept and a contemporary field of study and practice. The notion that true power and greatness comes from living one's life in service to others can be found in all the world's major religions. From Buddha's compassion for the sick and dying to Moses's defense of oppressed slaves to Jesus's mission to serve "the least among us," we find the value of serving others at the heart of spiritual traditions from the East and the West.

The modern incarnation of this concept can be traced to an essay published in 1970 by Robert K. Greenleaf called "The Servant as Leader." Greenleaf was a corporate executive who was deeply disturbed by the chaos and upheaval of the late 1960s. The Vietnam War was raging abroad, the US Government was in crisis as a result of the corruption and deception of the Watergate scandal, and chaos was erupting on college campuses across the country.

In other words, it was a time much like our own.

Greenleaf looked around and saw institutions and individuals who had lost the trust and respect of the wider public because they were so clearly driven by their own hungers for power, material gain, and self-preservation. His response was not to fall into despair, cynicism, or nihilism; it was to recognize that there was another model of leadership that we could look to that had the power to rebuild trust and respond meaningfully to the challenges of the day. He elevated the timeless concept of "servant as leader" as the path out of the darkness and chaos of the day.

According to Greenleaf, the heart of service was this: One's deepest motivation was to desire the development and well-being of others rather than oneself. Here's how he expressed this idea:

> *The best test [of servant leadership] is: Do those*
> *served grow as persons? Do they,* while being served,
> *become healthier, wiser, freer, more autonomous,*
> *more likely themselves to become servants? And,*
> *what is the effect on the least privileged in society?*
> *Will they benefit or at least not be further deprived?*
> *(Greenleaf, p. 27)*

Since Greenleaf published this essay, we've seen the emergence of a vast literature on the topic of servant leadership. You'll find dozens of books on the topic of servant leadership on Amazon, 1.2 million hits for the phrase on Google Scholar, and 200 million hits if you type the term into Google. The subject has been explored through a myriad of lenses including religious leadership, military leadership, public sector leadership, business leadership, and nonprofit leadership. Clearly, it's a popular topic that resonates widely in our world today.

This book does not seek to provide an overview of this vast literature. I'm not out to explore the philosophy of servant leadership as an intellectual exercise as readers seeking that kind of treatment of this subject can easily find that content elsewhere. This book accepts the basic principles of servant leadership already presented here:

Servant leaders are individuals who are focused on supporting and developing others, especially those who are marginalized and vulnerable. When they seek positions of power, authority, and influence, they do so out of a desire to expand their capacity to serve others rather than out of desires to feed personal hungers for power, adulation, or material gain. As a result of how they lead, they leave others healthier, wiser, more free, more autonomous, and more likely to themselves serve others.

Servant leaders stand in stark contrast to leaders who foster dependency, demand obedience, inflame polarization, and invite people to focus on stewing in their own grievances rather than on using their gifts to serve others. That kind of leader causes followers to question their own voice, abilities, and insights in ways that leave them less capable of moving forward on their own.

On the one hand, the concept of servant leadership couldn't be more simple. On the other hand, it's an approach to leadership with the potential to transform the world. Imagine a world where we saw this kind of leadership practiced by political leaders, business leaders, community leaders, and ordinary citizens on a daily basis! My hope is that this book might move us a bit closer to bringing that vision to life.

The other concept at the heart of this book is *"at scale."*

The concept of "at scale" means "at a size or number that makes it possible to meaningfully address the challenge at hand." Challenges like responding to the climate crisis, renewing democracy, or creating racial equity are complex public problems that affect all of our lives. It is clear that we cannot expect one or two heroic leaders to show up and magically solve these pressing public problems for us. Rather, we need vast numbers of individuals stepping up to address these issues skillfully in communities across the nation and the world. If we believe that servant leaders can play a vital role in our efforts to respond meaningfully to the challenges of this moment, then we need a lot of them.

This book presents a proven, tested approach to making that happen. As you'll see in the pages ahead, it took a long time to figure out an approach that worked. Along the way, I arrived at the following key insight: Creating an effective large-scale leadership development system is a different challenge from developing individual leaders or even small groups of leaders. When we seek to do this work at scale, we include but also transcend the work of individual and small group leadership development. We find ourselves confronting issues that are not readily apparent at the smaller scales, and we must shift our focus to different challenges and undertake different kinds of work.

As an Integral Master Coach, I've got a lot of training and experience in engaging effectively in one-on-one leadership development. I love the work of connecting deeply with a client and accompanying them on a personal journey of transformation. That training and experience informs the approach you'll encounter in this book in foundational ways.

As a leadership educator, I've also got a wealth of training and experience in leading rooms full of people through leadership trainings and workshops. That work is quite different from one-on-one coaching, but it is also work that I love to do. Creating a space in which dozens of individuals grapple deeply with the meaning and practice of leadership is a form of bliss for me. I've done it for years with thousands of groups at this point, and all that training and experience as a leadership educator informs this approach in foundational ways as well.

When we talk about developing servant leaders at scale, though, we arrive at a critical shift in the nature of the work we are doing. The individual and small group work is about *developing servant leaders*. When we seek to do this at scale, we shift to the challenge of *creating a servant leadership development system*. This is about building an organizational capacity to guide thousands of individuals through a powerful and personally meaningful leadership development experience, with consistency and excellence, year after year after year.

It turns out that organizations tend to resist the emergence of this capacity because it challenges some deeply held and largely unexamined assumptions about what leadership development means and how change happens. I've learned through personal experience that the effort to do this work at scale evokes a whole set of issues that must be addressed and challenges that must be overcome that are not apparent when engaging in the work of individual or small group leadership development. I've spent the last 20 years of my life figuring out how to understand and effectively address those challenges, and I've written this book to share what I've learned.

If you are seeking guidance on how to personally develop as a servant leader ("six key skills to become a servant leader" or "three daily practices to grow as a servant leader"), you are invited to look elsewhere, as there are a wealth of resources for individuals seeking that kind of content. If you are an organizational leader in a position to design and implement leadership development experiences for large numbers of individuals, I invite you to read on. If you are a philanthropist who recognizes that leadership development and communal impact are too interconnected to separate, you'll find the ideas presented here to be of interest as well.

MY BACKGROUND

There are six facets of my own background that inform this work in foundational ways: my experience with service programs, my academic studies, my career as an organizational leader in the world of service, my training as an Integral Master Coach, my identity, and my lifelong search for spiritual wisdom.

The first – and I believe the most important – perspective that I bring to this work is my many years of experience as both a participant and a staff member of long-term service programs. My first professional experience following college was to enroll as a participant on a ten-month service program in Israel. It was called *Project Otzma*, and I spent my days tutoring elementary school students in English, running after school programs, painting murals, working with Ethiopian and Russian immigrants, and engaging in educational seminars focused on the history and present-day issues of the region. My days were spent serving others and thinking deeply about the challenges of making the world a better place, and it was the happiest I'd ever been. Following that program, I returned to the United States for two years before returning as a staff member of the same program. I spent the next 10 months serving and supporting nearly 80 participants who themselves were serving others and had my first experiences trying to unleash the full leadership development potential of a demanding long-term service program.

I started graduate school in 1999 but spent my academic summers leading service trips. In 2002, I co-led a group of 15 Jewish college students on an international service trip with an organization called American Jewish World Service (AJWS); we spent five weeks in rural Honduras working alongside a local community to build an irrigation ditch that would bring fresh water to their village and then spent three weeks in Simferopol, Ukraine helping the local Jewish community clear out an overgrown Jewish cemetery in town. In the summer of 2003, I co-led another group of Jewish college students on a similar trip with AJWS. That summer, we spent five weeks in Ghana working with a rural village to build a new schoolhouse in their town, and then three weeks in Kharkov, Ukraine, again helping them to clear out an overgrown Jewish cemetery.

I spent my days working alongside marginalized and vulnerable communities in different parts of the world and engaged in intense discussions evoked by the challenges of seeking to serve others. How do we address the root causes of injustice and inequality? How do we serve others without creating dependency and passivity? How do we confront overwhelming social issues without tipping into despair? How do we grapple with our location in a complex social system that leaves us all privileged in some ways and oppressed in others?

It is hard for me to overstate how formative these service experiences have been in my life. Quite simply, I've learned that when I am in service to others, I experience spiritual peace. No matter how spartan and uncomfortable the living conditions may have been or how intense and demanding the manual labor was on those trips, I felt joy and contentment in my soul.

I also came to believe that service experiences are uniquely powerful contexts for learning and personal growth. At the risk of understatement, the experience of living and working alongside a community in rural Honduras is dramatically different from the experience of sitting in a classroom in the United States and discussing the history of central America, international development, or relationships between the global north and the Global South. On a service trip, you are immersed in a new reality, not just new ideas. You leave behind all that is familiar and comfortable and face daily challenges, questions, and struggles that have the potential to transform you at the deepest levels.

Those experiences led directly to my professional path, which involved a decade working in the national service movement, and seven years working to bring servant leaders into politics (more on that in a moment).

In terms of academic studies, I received my Doctorate of Education from the Harvard Graduate School of Education (HGSE) in 2005. I was enrolled in the Human Development and Psychology program at HGSE and I completed half of my course work at the Kennedy School of Government (KSG). At HGSE I was trained as a developmental psychologist; I studied theories and research related to moral development, cognitive development, adolescent development and more. At KSG, I was deeply immersed in the field of adaptive leadership,[1] an approach to leadership that integrates a highly psychological approach to individual behavior with a sophisticated understanding of how complex systems change or – more often – resist change.

My academic work represented an effort to maintain a dual focus on the inner life of individuals seeking to make positive change in the world while simultaneously staying focused on the larger systemic dynamics in which those individuals operated. In other words, I was striving to understand the relationship between the "micro" (the individual) and the "macro" (the system). My dissertation was a deep dive into that question, and I later had the chance to publish a revised version of that work as my first book, entitled *Race and Social Change: A Quest, A Study, A Call to Action* (Jossey Bass, 2017). For a brief overview of the ideas shared in that book, check out my 2011 TEDx talk entitled *Social Justice Leadership in Living Systems*.

Upon completing my doctorate, I chose to pursue a career in the nonprofit sector rather than academia. Although I loved the world of scholarship and research, I've always felt most at home in the world of service. I landed at City Year, an

---

1 The adaptive leadership model was developed by Harvard professor Ronald Heifetz. To learn more about this work, check out his books *Leadership Without Easy Answers (1994)* and *Leadership on the Line (2002)*.

education-focused AmeriCorps program based in Boston with sites in dozens of other cities across the nation. It was over the course of my 10 years at that national nonprofit that I developed frameworks at the heart of this book.

You'll learn a great deal more about my time at City Year in Chapters 1 and 2 of this book; for now, I'll just note that City Year gave me the chance to explore the work of developing servant leaders at scale. When I joined the organization, it engaged roughly 1,500 AmeriCorps members in service every year in 15 cities across the United States; by the time I left, a decade later it had grown to more than 2,500 AmeriCorps members in 25 cities. My work at that organization gave me the opportunity to refine an approach to effectively engage that number of individuals year after year.

After 10 years at City Year, I joined a start-up organization called the New Politics Leadership Academy (NPLA). NPLA is a bi-partisan nonprofit whose mission is to revitalize American democracy by recruiting and developing servant leaders who put country and community over self. The visionary founder, Emily Cherniack, was a fellow City Year alum whose mission is to bring more servant leaders – military veterans and alumni of national service programs like AmeriCorps and Peace Corps – into politics. I spent the next seven years using the approaches to leadership development described in this book to recruit and develop servant leaders ready to answer the call to serve again through electoral politics. In just those few years, we grew from a staff of two to 18 employees and have graduated more than 2,500 individuals from our leadership development programs. As of this writing, we have dozens of alumni serving in elected office at every level from school board to Congress.

In addition, this work is deeply informed by my training as an Integral Master Coach, trained by Integral Coaching Canada.[2] This type of coaching is grounded in the work of Ken Wilber, a towering intellect of our era whose life's work involved pulling together an astonishing array of theories related to human development from both the West and the East and integrating them into one coherent conceptual model. The founders of Integral Coaching Canada found a way to turn this rigorous intellectual framework into a practical, effective approach to coaching that focuses on guiding clients through shifts in their innermost ways of being. Through years of training and work with many clients, I've developed a sophisticated understanding of how to support individuals in moving through this kind of deep inner transformation.

In terms of identity, I'm a cis-gendered, straight, white, Jewish male. I grew up middle class and currently live with my wife and two children in a suburb of Boston. I've done a lot of work to understand the ways that my perspective and insights are inevitably influenced and limited in meaningful ways by these aspects of my identity. I share my personal journey around these issues in detail in my first book, *Race and Social Change*. Anyone who is interested in learning more about how my identity informs my approach to leadership development is welcome to check out that earlier book. For now, I'll just say this: I recognize that I'll always be on a journey of learning and discovery around matters of race and social change, and I commit to staying humble, curious, and open to feedback and new learnings as I walk the path. I strive to live by Maya Angelou's well-known advice: "Do the best you can until you know better. Then when you know better, do better."

---

2 Learn more at www.integralcoachingcanada.com

Finally, I am a devotee of personal growth experiences, a passionate student of Joseph Campbell and the field of comparative mythology, and a lifelong spiritual seeker. All of those interests inform this work in clear and powerful ways. This book will surely be of interest to any readers who are committed to walking the path of personal development and spiritual growth and are curious about how we might invite large numbers of individuals into a meaningful process of personal transformation.

ROADMAP FOR THE JOURNEY

Here's what you'll find in the pages ahead:

Chapters 1 and 2 tell the story of developing a powerful, scalable approach to cultivating inner development among the corps members and staff at City Year, a national nonprofit addressing America's high school drop-out crisis. These chapters describe the years of trial and error, failure, experimentation, and innovation that went into developing and refining an approach to leadership development called *The Flame* and *The Journey*. Over the course of these chapters, you'll gain a clear understanding of the problems solved by this method and the strategic value of this approach.

The next three chapters explore the different elements of *The Flame* model of leadership development. Chapter 3 illuminates the power of having a strong organizational culture and values. Chapter 4 discusses the "Do" and "Know" elements of *The Flame*, which focus on work experiences as well as knowledge, skills, and training. Chapter 5 presents a deep dive into the innermost "Be" level of *The Flame*, describing how to guide individuals through a journey toward inner clarity and integrity in powerful and sophisticated ways.

In Chapter 6, we highlight a skill that has proven to be essential to the practice of using this approach to leadership development: *Question Formulation*. This methodology provided a breakthrough moment in the effort to create a powerful, scalable reflection experience. This chapter explains what question finding is, how it works, and why it is essential.

In Chapter 7, we explore how this work has been utilized by the NPLA. The *Flame* and *Journey* work is central to NPLA's strategy and programming, and this chapter presents an example of what it looks like to have this approach integrated into an organization from its founding.

Finally, in Chapter 8, we conclude with a brief exploration of the Inner Development Goals (IDGs), an international movement to bring a clear and rigorous focus on inner development to organizations, communities, and nations seeking to address public challenges. We'll explore how the Flame and Journey work described in this book is both a manifestation of and a contribution to that emerging movement. We'll end with a discussion of why this focus on inner development is so essential at this moment of "poli-crisis," when we face so many overlapping and interconnected crises unfolding simultaneously.

WHO IS THIS BOOK FOR?

The primary audience for this book is senior leaders at organizations that are focused on developing servant leaders at scale. This includes nonprofit leaders at organizations that are similar to City Year and the NPLA in that they engage large numbers of participants in service-related fields, and they recognize the need to offer all of those individuals a powerful and transformational leadership development experience.

More specifically, this book is for those senior leaders who are responsible for designing and delivering leadership development programming at those organizations.

The secondary audience for this book is funders and philanthropists who recognize the need to recruit and develop leaders who are willing and able to confront the pressing public problems of our day and aspire to do that work at scale. In recent years, the philanthropic community has grown increasingly cognizant of the fact that efforts to address critical issues with a narrow focus on outcomes and metrics are inevitably limited in impact and effectiveness. The most strategic approach is to integrate a rigorous focus on impact with a thoughtful and intentional approach to developing the individuals working at the grassroots or front lines to create that impact. Funders and philanthropists seeking ways to do that powerfully and at scale will find much that is of interest in the pages ahead.

A third audience for this book is scholars and practitioners seeking to advance the IDGs. The IDGs are a complement to the Sustainable Development Goals (SDGs) created by the United Nations. The SDGs are a collection of 17 clear goals related to social and economic development; examples include ending hunger and poverty, providing access to clean water, and a quality education around the world. The SDGs were designed to focus global international development efforts on clear goals to be achieved by 2030. Recognizing that progress needed to be accelerated, a group of thought leaders launched the parallel initiative of IDGs. These highlight a related set of inner capacities that we need to develop individually and collectively in order to better address public problems in effective and sustainable ways. Individuals who are interested in effectively integrating a dual focus on sustainable development and inner development will appreciate the insights in the pages ahead.

Finally, a fourth audience for this book is academics and scholars with an interest in leadership development. As a result of my academic background, I bring an in-depth knowledge of literature and research related to leadership, social change, adult development, and organizational design to this work. Although this book is primarily written as a guide for practitioners, scholars will find that this book offers considerable theoretical substance and depth and is of interest as an effort to develop practical, scalable applications of leadership theory.

WHY WE NEED SERVANT LEADERS

Robert Greenleaf's test of servant leadership is clear and straightforward: *Do those served become healthier, wiser, freer, more autonomous, more likely themselves to become servants?* It is maddeningly, alarmingly easy to find examples of leaders who fail that test right now. In the political world, authoritarians are on the rise here in the United States and abroad. They demand obedience, spread ignorance and encourage followers to rage at "the other" rather than serve the marginalized and vulnerable. In the field of technology, it is clear that leaders have intentionally created products that cultivate addiction, corrode mental health, and amplify anxiety and feelings of loneliness among billions of users. Everywhere we look, we see leaders who leave followers sicker, more ignorant, more dependent, and more focused on their own hungers and grievances than on serving others.

The sheer amount of bad news is hard to process, and it's easy to become cynical or hopeless in the face of the toxicity we see all around us. It's important to realize, though, that the darkness is not the whole story.

Over the course of my career at City Year and at the NPLA, I've had the honor and privilege to spend my days with some of the remarkable servant leaders stepping up to lead at every level across our nation. Every year, City Year engages thousands of young adults who have chosen to spend ten-hour days serving as tutors, mentors and role models to kids in high-need schools. At NPLA, I worked with some of the military vets, returned Peace Corps volunteers, educators, healthcare workers, and public servants who have been serving for years and are seriously considering stepping into the arena to serve again through politics.

At NPLA, we often say that the lack of servant leaders in our politics is not the result of a lack of servant leaders in our nation. There are vast numbers of these remarkable souls living lives of genuine service. They are already leading in their communities and organizations, doing what they can to use their gifts to support and develop others. I've come to believe that these servant leaders are a precious national resource; a source of energy that could be cultivated and channeled in ways that transform the world. The question is whether we can serve *them* meaningfully and at a scale that is commensurate with the challenges we face today.

I believe we can. At this critical moment that is so fraught with danger, I believe that we must. If you are interested in learning how to make that happen, I invite you to read on.

1

THE JOURNEY TO THE JOURNEY

> *Simple can be harder than complex: You have to*
> *work hard to get your thinking clean to make it*
> *simple. But it's worth it in the end because once you*
> *get there, you can move mountains.* – Steve Jobs
> (1998)

It was the informational interview that changed my life.

I was a newly minted Doctor of Education on the hunt for a job. The focus of my studies had been youth civic leadership education, and a colleague encouraged me to connect with his daughter, who worked at a Boston-based nonprofit called City Year. I met her at the City Year offices, and after about 30 minutes, she walked me over to the office of the Vice President of Research for the organization. He was a fellow Harvard Graduate School of Education alum, and we spent an enjoyable 20 minutes talking about his work at City Year and my recently completed studies.

Two days later, the VP called to say that City Year wanted to fly me to DC to be a part of their upcoming Thought Leader meeting. Soon after that, I found myself employed as City Year's Senior Manager of Research and Evaluation. It was an unexpected opportunity, and I had no idea that it was the beginning of a journey that would become the focus of my professional life for the next decade.

City Year is an AmeriCorps program that engages young adult Corps Members – ages 17–24 – in a year of full-time service. Founded in 1988 as a 50-person pilot program in Boston, the organization now has sites in 29 US cities and engages more than 2,000 AmeriCorps members each year; it also has international affiliates in Johannesburg, South Africa as well as in London, Birmingham, and Manchester, United Kingdom. It is one of the most successful and high-performing nonprofits in the nation, and it has catalyzed a national and global service movement that continues to grow and evolve to this day.

Today, City Year is fully focused on addressing America's high school drop-out crisis; all its AmeriCorps members serve in high-need schools in a strategic and data-driven effort to keep kids in school and on track to graduate. Back when I was first hired in 2006, however, the organization was just beginning to make the pivot to this focus on education. In those days, City Year AmeriCorps members were involved in all kinds of service, from cleaning parks and painting murals to running weekend youth leadership programs to running after school activities. The journey described in the pages ahead unfolded as City Year was engaged in the major organizational change effort of focusing all its efforts on addressing the high-school drop-out crisis.

City Year was already 18 years old by the time I joined the organization. Its full history is a fascinating story of organizational growth and impact, as well as a window into the evolution of America's modern national service movement. That full history is beyond the scope of this book and is not my tale to tell. The story of the development of the Flame and Journey approach to leadership development is a small piece of City Year's development, and it reflects the focus of the work I was engaged in during my decade at the organization.

Soon after I began working at City Year, I came to some realizations about how I might make a meaningful contribution to the organization's approach to leadership development. First, the organization lacked a powerful, substantive approach to reflection that gave every AmeriCorps member a chance to reflect deeply on the uniquely personal meaning of their service experience. The story of innovating around an effective and scalable approach to transformational reflection is the story of the Journey. Second, the organization lacked a clear and comprehensive conceptual model of leadership development that honored the unique nature of national service as a context for leadership development. The story of developing that conceptual model is the story of the Flame.

In the next two chapters, I share the stories of the two intertwined efforts that led to the innovations at the heart of this book.

THE QUEST FOR A SCALABLE REFLECTION PROCESS

Since its founding, City Year has always appreciated the value of reflection. In the early years, Corps Members would spend Monday through Thursday engaged in community service work, and Fridays were reserved as Leadership Development Days (LDDs), in which Corps Members engaged in service-related trainings, community building activities, and reflection experiences. Colleagues on staff who were around in those early years told stories of days when something difficult would happen in a community (for example, the closing of a school) and the entire corps would take a day off from service to come together for hours of dialogue and reflection to process the news.

Again, I joined the organization at a moment when it was refocusing its service model to address the high school drop-out crisis. The service model became much more focused in ways that required AmeriCorps members to provide rigorous academic and social support to students in high-need schools. The academic focus required more time for training in service-related skills like how to engage in effective literacy tutoring, math support, and behavior management. It also involved a rigorous focus on measurement, and that work required time dedicated to data collection, entry, and analysis.

As the service model grew ever more sophisticated, the demands on AmeriCorps members' time expanded. City Year's appreciation for reflection remained, but the rigor of the new service model fundamentally transformed the AmeriCorps member experience and the time available to pause and reflect on a consistent basis. By the time I joined the organization, time available for reflection had shrunk dramatically. City Year had retained a commitment to debriefing programs, so you could regularly find AmeriCorps members gathered together immediately following, say, an afterschool event to do a quick "Plus/Delta" debrief to discuss what had gone well and what could have been improved about the event. And there were still Friday LDDs although these usually only happened every other week, and much of the time was focused on service-related training. Also, these days often included a session focused on relevant social issues like educational inequality or the impact of trauma on child development.

The reflection experiences that remained at City Year were valuable, but they were limited. Opportunities for AmeriCorps members to pause, briefly turn away from the demands of service, and turn inwards to explore the uniquely personal meaning of their intense daily service experiences were increasingly rare. While some AmeriCorps members surely explored those issues in conversations on the way to work in the morning or while walking down the halls of a school with a teammate, the organization had no consistent, systemic, and powerful approach to supporting AmeriCorps members in staying present and awake to the uniquely personal inner dimension of their service journey.

Of course, there was nothing unusual about the lack of reflection opportunities at City Year. Very few organizations prioritize time for that kind of inner work. To my knowledge, no organization operating anywhere near the size and scale of City Year had an approach to integrating consistent, deep, and personal reflection into the workday.

For a variety of reasons, I believed deeply that this was problematic.

First, I was both a participant and staff alum of an intense ten-month service program, and I knew how transformational the experience could be. The experience of serving others, confronting major social issues, and working on a diverse team, all while navigating the uncertainty of young adulthood is profoundly complex. I knew from personal experience how easy it was to settle into a myopic focus on the next item on the to-do list while losing touch with the deeper meaning and impact of each day.

Second, as an introvert, I was a keen observer of my own inner processes and struggles over the course of my service experiences. After leading service trips in Israel, Ghana, Honduras, and Ukraine, I understood that different individuals on a service trip focus on different aspects of the experience. Some love building relationships with those they serve; others are fascinated by the larger social issues encountered in this work; others pay attention to the group dynamics within the team delivering the service. As for myself, I have always been drawn inwards; I was fascinated and challenged by the inner work demanded by the choice to live a life of service to others. How do you serve others while still taking care of yourself? How do you work on the front lines of major social injustices without falling into despair? How do you navigate the feelings evoked by encountering your own privilege, or your own oppression? I knew for myself that it took years of ongoing reflection, study, and dialogue to live my way into personally meaningful answers to these questions, and it was problematic to expect AmeriCorps members to figure this all out in the spaces between tutoring time, training activities, and data entry sessions.

Finally, I had just completed a doctorate focused on leadership development, and my academic work had only reinforced my belief in not just the value but the necessity of reflection in the process of developing leaders. I learned that any leader seeking to confront a complex public problem must learn how to cycle between "getting on the dance floor," taking action and making things happen, and "getting to the balcony," stepping back to reflect on what is happening both around and within the self (Heifetz, 1994). I learned that at some point, every individual seeking to create change hits the limits of what they can accomplish at their own current level of development; if they want to increase their impact, they must turn inwards and develop themselves, essentially growing beyond their previous limitations. I personally experienced the truth of this insight, as semester after semester while at school I again and again confronted beliefs, assumptions, and ways of being that created problems around me...and then watched those problems resolve as I arrived at more advanced and evolved ways of being with the world around and within myself.

For all these reasons, I had arrived at a simple, immutable assertion: *You cannot develop leaders without reflection.* If City Year wanted to measurably reduce America's high school drop-out crisis, it could not let the many very real demands of delivering a sophisticated and high-stakes service model crowd out the time for deep personal growth and development for both AmeriCorps members and staff. Within my first months at the organization, I realized that the development of some kind of powerful approach to reflection – integrated into the workday – would be my contribution to City Year.

There was one catch: I had no idea how to do it.

While I had plenty of experience with reflection, personal growth, and inner work, all of these experiences happened in academia, in small-group retreats, or through one-on-one interactions. I had never encountered this kind of work integrated into the workday of a large-scale organization. I spent months looking for other organizations that had figured this out and found no models that approached the combination of depth and scale I hoped to achieve.

The closest effort I found was an organization called the Civic Reflection Project, and their model involved providing short readings related to service that AmeriCorps members could read and discuss in small groups. While there was surely value to that approach, it was grounded in a pedagogical approach I preferred to avoid. I didn't want to invite people to reflect on *readings,* in the hopes they would frequently end up making useful connections to their own lives. I wanted people to reflect *directly on themselves*. Ultimately, I realized that this was not going to be a process of importing a fully developed model from another organization into City Year; this was going to be a process of innovating our way toward creating something that didn't exist anywhere else.

As I contemplated this undertaking, I was clear about a few things:

First, the challenge here was not really about developing leaders; it was about creating and refining a *leadership development system*. Whatever emerged from this process would have to work at the scale of City Year (thousands of AmeriCorps members working across dozens of locations) and would have to be cooked into the organizational culture in ways that ensured that it would endure year after year.

Second, this effort could not rely on external consultants. It was both prohibitively expensive and logistically untenable to try to recruit and deploy external consultants to lead reflection experiences across dozens of sites multiple times a year. We had to find a way to empower existing staff to create these experiences for their colleagues while still executing on all their other important responsibilities. Essentially, this would involve creating a new organizational capacity within City Year to create reflection spaces for itself at scale on a consistent basis.

Finally, given these constraints, any model we arrived at had to be deep and powerful enough to produce genuine transformation, yet simple enough to be led by current staff who were not highly trained facilitators. We had to find a way to empower hundreds of talented nonexperts to create meaningful experiences for thousands of peers and colleagues.

With this clarity in mind, I took the first steps along the path toward what would become the Journey.

The first challenge was very clear: Open up time and space for reflection within the workday for AmeriCorps members. Resistance was intense, with the same message coming from stakeholders all across the organization: *It's nice to have a chance to reflect, but we've got way too much other important stuff to do to make time for that.* Literally nobody asserted that reflection was a bad idea or not valuable, but given the urgency of the work, the sophistication of the service model, and the need to achieve measurable impact and report on that impact to multiple stakeholders, reflection simply was never the top priority. Across the organization, even staff who were sympathetic to the vision asserted that there was simply too much other important stuff to do to make this happen.

We soon proved that assertion to be wrong. After months of dialogue and discussion, I was given the opportunity to pilot a reflection experience that would be integrated into the workday for AmeriCorps members. It began as a limited pilot, in which I was able to facilitate discussions with a group of Senior Corps Members (second year AmeriCorps members who helped provide support and guidance to first year AmeriCorps members). Based on that small pilot, we moved to a larger pilot, involving the full corps at five of City Year's 17 sites. We were given a chance to put a one-hour bi-weekly small group reflection session on the calendar during Friday LDDs, when AmeriCorps members spent time on training, education, and team-building activities. We empowered Senior Corps Members to facilitate these sessions. We got sessions scheduled, and most of the time they happened as planned.

While it was exciting to see that it actually was possible to make time for reflection, there was one very big problem: Most people *hated* these reflection sessions.

We learned that many of the individuals felt that they were being forced to reflect, and they resented the pressure. We heard that many of these discussions devolved into venting sessions in which discussion focused more on voicing complaints and frustrations than on engaging in productive dialogue; participants said these spaces were corroding morale and undermining idealism. Also, we heard that conversations often focused on matters that were trivial and unimportant. For example, one group chose to discuss what radio station they should listen to on the shared 20-minute car ride to the service site. As a result, there was a general sense that these sessions were a waste of time, especially when compared to all the other vital work that needed to get done.

City Year has an annual AmeriCorps member end-of-year survey, and that year's survey included questions about the reflection program. The results were, let's just say, under-whelming: Only 47% of AmeriCorps members who had participated in the program were "satisfied" or "highly satisfied" with the program. The majority of participants hated it.

The organization has a strong commitment to learning from data, and one of the most difficult days of my career was the day that I had to present these results to my supervisor and colleagues at our annual data review meeting. This program was not working, and my supervisor could have easily pulled the plug on the initiative right then. To her great credit, she allowed the experiment to continue, giving me time and space to figure out how to make this work.

One of the reasons why the program was allowed to continue was the fact that there was one bright spot in the data: The satisfaction rating at one of the pilot sites – City Year New Hampshire (CYNH) – was in the 80 percentile range. Thanks to the leadership of a charismatic and deeply thoughtful staff person named Bobby Kessling, the majority of AmeriCorps members at our New Hampshire site found this space to be valuable and productive. CYNH proved that it was possible to make reflection work; the challenge was to figure out what they were doing right and scale it across the entire organization.

One clear learning from the pilot was the importance of having a site-level staff person who was a genuine champion of this work. Bobby was a true believer in the importance of reflection, and the AmeriCorps members at his site engaged with this work in ways that mirrored Bobby's own enthusiasm.

At other locations, the site-level leaders for this initiative were, comparatively speaking, lukewarm supporters who approached this more as a requirement to implement an initiative of interest to HQ than as a chance to engage

AmeriCorps members in a transformational development experience. Again, the AmeriCorps members at those sites engaged with the work in ways that mirrored those leaders' own attitudes toward the initiative.

Clearly, this work could not be managed like a technical solution, in which HQ shared the model, supported implementation, and checked for compliance. Somehow, the attitude the entire site took toward this work reflected the inner orientation of the local staff lead, and HQ's ability to influence that deeply personal attitude toward this work was very limited. It very quickly became clear it was far more strategic to find a local leader for this work who had enthusiasm and passion rather than positional power. When it came to creating powerful reflection experiences across the site, a Senior Corps Member with a genuine love of reflection was a more effective lead than a Program Director (a role several levels higher up on the org chart) who viewed this work as just another initiative to manage.

This insight had clear strategic implications. In the years ahead, we focused more on identifying individuals at any level of the organization with a passion for reflection and personal growth than on trying to manage this through the organizational hierarchy. We had many sites where a front-line staff person led this work powerfully, successfully integrating a consistent reflection practice into the culture at the site despite having minimal positional power. This was about growing the community of human beings willing to champion this work at all levels of the organization, not managing the hierarchy to ensure employees complied with requirements set forth by HQ.

Another clear learning was that our model needed a lot of work. Simply opening up a space and providing a lightly trained facilitator was not effective; we had to find ways to invite people into this work without triggering widespread resentment and resistance, and we needed to develop approaches that ensured that conversations in these spaces were productive and valuable rather than negative and trivial. And so, we began experimenting.

An early focus was on developing a curriculum originally called the City Year Personal Leadership Development Workbook. The workbook presented a sequence of leadership development-related reflection exercises that AmeriCorps members would complete and discuss in these spaces. The exercises included activities like crafting a personal leadership mission statement, developing a list of core values, and identifying a personal "dragon to slay" – a fear or obstacle that one had to confront to enhance one's leadership impact. With each year that passed, we were able to refine the wording, sequence, and timing of these activities so that they landed in the right way and at the right moment in the AmeriCorps experience and effectively engaged participants in important inner work.

Another early focus was on integrating Joseph Campbell's "Hero's Journey" framework into the curriculum. I'll have a lot more to say about Campbell in Chapter Five, but for now a quick summary will suffice. Campbell was a comparative mythologist who studied myths told all around the world; in a seminal book published in 1948 called *The Hero with a Thousand Faces*, he laid out his profound insight that at the heart of thousands of seemingly disparate myths from around the world was a single, universal story that he called the *Hero's Journey*. At its most basic, the Journey involves leaving behind a familiar, comfortable world and stepping into the unknown, confronting a series of trials and tests that transform the self, and then using the gifts of that journey to serve others.

In the late 1980s, Campbell was interviewed by Bill Moyers for a PBS series called *The Power of Myth*; City Year co-founder Michael Brown has said many times that watching that series and encountering Campbell's ideas was one of the key experiences that inspired him to found the organization. He and co-founder Alan Khazei believed that a year of service could serve as a sort of "civic rite of passage" – a transformational experience that could create generations of engaged, informed, and responsible citizens.

In a meaningful sense, Campbell's ideas were cooked into the DNA of City Year. They also had a profound impact on my own life prior to joining the organization (for reasons I'll explain in more detail in Chapter Five). For both of these reasons, I was excited about integrating elements of the Hero's Journey model into this reflection curriculum. So, we gave that a try... and once again failed epically.

While Campbell's Hero's Journey framework can be reduced to the three stages of Departure, Road of Trials, Return, the full model is much more detailed. It includes a cycle of 12 different experiences, with names like "Questioning the Call," "Crossing the First Threshold," "Meeting the Mentor," and "The Belly of the Whale." In my enthusiasm for Campbell's work, I tried to cram all of this down the throats of AmeriCorps members, challenging them to reflect on when in their City Year they experienced, say, "questioning the call" or "entering the belly of the whale. While a small handful of AmeriCorps members across the organization loved this stuff, the vast majority found the whole thing to be corny, esoteric, and deeply irrelevant to the work of tutoring and mentoring their students. The resistance to these activities was so intense that I wondered if future efforts could ever undo the negativity generated by these experiences.

Once again, though, I was allowed to continue experimenting despite the overwhelming evidence that what we were doing wasn't working.

The next year, we dialed the Campbell content way, way back. We shared the model in its most basic three-stage form and offered it as an overarching metaphor for understanding the year ahead. Because the framing of a year of service as a transformational civic rite of passage was already a part of the organizational culture, this revised approach helped this work to feel more authentic and integral to City Year. It also had the effect of inviting each individual AmeriCorps member to think about the deeper dimensions of their service experiences without triggering the kind of allergic reaction generated by the heavy-handed programming we tried the year before.

While that first approach to Campbell was a disaster, this revised approach resonated powerfully with organizational culture. The next year, we decided to rename our leadership curriculum; it would no longer be called the *City Year Personal Leadership Development Workbook*; it would become *The Idealist's Journey: The City Year Leadership Development Guide and Workbook*. The new name referenced Campbell's work while adapting it in subtle but meaningful ways. The notion of idealism was central to everything City Year did, and the concept of "hero" evoked for many an archetype of a lone masculine warrior (think Rambo or John Wayne) that was anathema to an organization so committed to both teamwork and empathy. In naming the curriculum *The Idealist's Journey*, we honored Campbell's influence while adapting it to align with the organizational culture in vital ways. With the new title, a key piece of the puzzle fell into place.

There were still, however, pockets of intense resistance to this work among the thousands of AmeriCorps members we aspired to develop with this curriculum each year. I did a lot of site visits, focus groups, individual conversations, and reviewing of evaluation data in those early years and came to learn that this reflection work generated a predictable pattern of responses at the majority of sites across the City Year network. A minority of AmeriCorps members – roughly 10% –

LOVED IJ (as the Idealist's Journey quickly came to be known). From what I could tell, these were introverts with a passion for reflection who found immense value in having this space to turn inwards on a consistent basis over the course of the year. Some of these individuals made it clear that the IJ was their favorite part of their City Year experience. Then, a clear majority – roughly 80% – were lukewarm about the program. They understood that reflection could be useful and found some value in the chance to connect with peers and think about their own development. They didn't love the experience, but they didn't hate it either; they responded to this work with a range of emotions somewhere between mild enjoyment and patient tolerance.

Then, there were the haters.

Another minority – that final 10% – HATED IJ. They found the whole concept of forced reflection to be offensive and deeply patronizing. They made it clear that they knew how to reflect in their own ways and on their own time, and they were absolutely certain that their time could be better spent doing basically anything else besides sitting in a circle talking about values or dragons to slay. A few of these folks made it clear that IJ was easily the worst part of their City Year.

A major challenge to this work was the fact that this small minority of haters clearly had a significant – and notably negative – impact on the experience of all the other AmeriCorps members. At its best, this kind of reflection work made possible a degree of openness and vulnerability that allowed for deeply meaningful dialogue among AmeriCorps members. But the dynamics and quality of group presence that allowed for this kind of openness was remarkably fragile. If just one individual in a group of 15 participants was vocally negative and intensely dismissive of the work, the quality of learning for that entire group was drastically diminished. When it came to reflection, it really was the case that one resistant Ameri-Corps member could diminish the power and value of this space, week after week after week.

This was a major problem for this effort to create reflection at scale, and I honestly had no idea how to solve it. If this was a small undertaking, I would consider telling individuals who did not like the IJ to just sit it out so others could make use of the space. But in an organization with thousands of Ameri-Corps members gathered in hundreds of groups across dozens of sites, making a policy saying that anyone who doesn't like this stuff could just opt out was likely de facto ending the program for all but the most committed and enthusiastic participants. We either had to find a way to make this work at scale, or make it go away.

At this point in the process, I was being supervised by Charlie Rose, a Senior VP who had been around since the founding of the organization. He was a master youth worker and community builder, and he was a true believer in the power and value of this work. At a time when chatter about the limitations of the Idealist's Journey could be heard among AmeriCorps members across the network, Charlie's support for the work never wavered. Over the years, he was an invaluable partner and champion for this effort as we continued to innovate our way toward a truly powerful and effective approach.

Around this time when I was feeling utterly lost about how to solve the current problems with the IJ, a guide appeared and illuminated the path forward in a manner that would have made Joseph Campbell smile. I had the remarkable honor of being invited to participate in a two-day leadership conference at the Harvard Business School. There were only 40 participants, and among them were the biggest names in the field. I felt a bit like a music fan getting to spend two days with my favorite rock stars; I couldn't believe I was in a room with these folks.

At one point, I had a chance to have a conversation with one of the globally recognized leadership experts in attendance. We were paired up and invited to reflect on a meaningful leadership challenge together. I told partner a bit about the work we were doing at City Year, and the challenge we were facing with the small but very vocal minority of individuals who resisted and resented reflection and were effectively destroying the value of the experience for all involved. His response provided an insight that was key to getting past this existential challenge to the work.

"*Jiu Jitsu*," he said.

> *You need to use the principles of* Jiu Jitsu. *The harder you push against that resistance, the stronger the resistance will become. So you need to not challenge it, but work with it, and find ways to redirect that energy and momentum in ways that strengthen your efforts.*

He was right. Our approach to the IJ up to that point was that reflection was something that you HAD to do, and if you refused you were not following the rules of the organization and were – essentially – a "bad" AmeriCorps member (at least in this space). The more we tried to demand compliance, the stronger and more entrenched the resistance became. My reflection partner's wisdom suggested another path.

The next year, we tried a very different approach. While being physically present at IJ was still required, we made a major shift from "We demand that you reflect" to "We invite you to reflect." We introduced IJ as follows:

> *We see a year of national service as a transformational rite of passage, and we know that giving you a chance*

to reflect on a consistent basis can help you stay present to the deeper dimensions of experiences this year. We invite you to undertake this inner journey this year, but we can't – and won't – force anyone to reflect. If you prefer not to reflect, we honor and respect that decision; we just request that you respect your colleagues and allow them to do this work.

That next year, all that intense, noisy resistance disappeared. That 10% of AmeriCorps members who actively disliked reflection were still there, but with the pressure to obey and comply removed, the resistance went away. Instead of vocally opposing this work, they quietly tolerated the time spent on IJ and allowed it to unfold around them. Their less-than-positive attitudes still influenced the group dynamics to some degree, but annoyed tolerance was far less disruptive than vocal rebellion. Remarkably, as the year went on we began to hear stories of IJ haters becoming IJ fans. All across the network, I began to hear from AmeriCorps members who said "At first I thought this IJ stuff was a total waste of time. But after seeing how helpful it was for others in my group, I decided to give it a try. Now I love it and get so much value from being able to slow down and think about my service experience in this way. Thanks for giving us the chance to do this work!"

My reflection partner was right: The principles of Jiu Jitsu worked. Thanks to his insight, a key obstacle to creating a successful large-scale reflection experience was overcome.

While it was exciting to see pieces of the puzzle falling into place, we weren't out of the woods yet. Parts of the program still weren't working, and our efforts to innovate and experiment were not effective.

For example, the vision for this work was that AmeriCorps members would gather in small groups for an hour, and that time would be dedicated to two main tasks: Workbook reflection and reflection on service-based experiences. The workbook was designed to guide AmeriCorps members through a series of important reflection questions focused on leadership development like developing a mission statement, clarifying their core values, and identifying a personal "dragon to slay." Knowing that AmeriCorps members were too busy to do homework, we gave them 8–10 minutes during IJ time to engage in this reflection and then 20 minutes to discuss it as a group. Each year, we listened carefully to feedback from across the network and found ways to make the language and the timing of these exercises a bit more resonant and powerful.

The second 30 minutes of each IJ session, though, was supposed to provide a chance for someone in the group to ask a question, raise an issue, or request guidance on a service-related challenge. The group would then have time to think deeply about a matter brought to the group by a fellow member of the group. The goal of this was to make sure that these discussions were meaningful and relevant for AmeriCorps members, and to give them a consistent space to explore their own questions with each other.

While we were able to make progress on the curriculum that was the focus of the first half of each IJ session, we were having real problems making sure that the second half of each hour was powerful and productive. We learned that sometimes AmeriCorps members would bring questions or issues that were really compelling and engaging; when that happened, members of the group loved the session and begged for time to continue the conversation when the formal hour of IJ came to a close. Just as often, though, AmeriCorps members would bring to their group matters that either weren't clearly presented or weren't really compelling. When groups didn't really know what they were supposed to be discussing, or nobody in the group felt that the issue was all that important, participants felt the IJ was a waste of time. They were adamant – and rightly so – that there were better ways to spend their time than having unfocused conversations or debating trivialities.

The challenge, then, was clear: How could we ensure that AmeriCorps members showed up at IJ sessions ready to share matters that were clear, compelling and important? At that time, all we could do was just hope it happened; surely there was a better way.

Our early efforts to support AmeriCorps members in this work focused on creating some structure and clarity around what they could bring into this space. We arrived at a model in which IJ participants were invited to bring presentations to their group based on one of the following three categories:

(1) *Service-Related Challenge:* Share a specific challenge you are encountering in your service work and the group will help you explore potential ways to address it.

(2) *Current Event:* Discuss a current event that is important to you (for example, the closing of a school in the district, violence in the community, a recent event in the community).

(3) *Big Question:* A philosophical issue raised by engaging in service (for example, "What does it mean to be a good person? Why is there so much injustice in the world?")

This structure was helpful in providing some guidance and clarity to AmeriCorps members thinking about what to bring to their IJ sessions. But we were still hearing lots of stories about IJ sessions feeling unfocused and only marginally productive. Sometimes, individuals would introduce these issues with rambling, unfocused explanations that filled 15–20 minutes of the 30-minute reflection time. Sometimes, an AmeriCorps member would invite the group to discuss a service-related challenge in very general terms ("Behavior management is hard!") and then much of the group's time would be spent trying to get at the element of this general challenge that was most important to the presenter.

This effort to bring some structure to the reflection space was good, but it wasn't great. It was increasingly apparent that clear, concise, and compelling presentations produced engaging and productive sessions that were highly valued by participants; unclear and unfocused presentations led to unfocused and low-energy discussions that just left everyone feeling that the session was a waste of time. Once again, we had hit an obstacle to achieving excellence in this work that I didn't know how to move beyond.

And once again, a guide appeared at just the right moment.

I had the privilege of participating in a program called *Selah*, a year-long leadership development fellowship for Jewish professionals working on social justice issues. Through that program I met Dan Rothstein, co-founder of a remark-able Boston-based nonprofit called *The Right Question Institute*. Dan and his co-founder, Luz Santana, had spent the last 20 years figuring out how to help marginalized commu-nities advocate for themselves by learning how to figure out the most strategic and personally meaningful questions to ask when engaging with schools, hospitals, local government, and other institutions in their communities. By the time that I met Dan, he and Luz had distilled decades of effort into a five-step process called Question Formulation Technique, and they were now focused on teaching educators to use the process with students.

Dan was excited to pilot bringing the work to City Year AmeriCorps members, who were all working in high-need schools. I loved the idea, and committed to finding a City Year site that was willing to let Dan and Luz run a training for their corps. CYNH jumped at the opportunity, and we scheduled a time for the training. Once again, CYNH was leading the network in the effort to take our reflection work to new levels.

On the day of the training, I made the trip to Manchester, New Hampshire to observe and learn. Dan and Luz presented a seemingly simple five-step process that involved selecting a topic to focus on, generating a wide-ranging list of questions related to that topic, and then thoughtfully selecting the question that invited exploration of that topic in ways that were most important and compelling. The product of this process was a brief (usually only two sentence) statement that succinctly presented an issue that was important to a particular AmeriCorps member, followed by a clear question. Here are some examples:

> *My student can't focus during our math tutoring sessions. What are best practices in keeping students engaged?*

> *The principal at my school was just replaced. What can we do to support students through this transition?*

> *My parents don't understand my choice to serve. How can I help them see the value of this experience?*

Watching this training unfold, I quickly grasped the power of this methodology. These statements may seem incredibly basic and direct, but it took some deep thinking, dialogue, and discussion to arrive at this level of clarity. The apparent simplicity of this five-step process is deceptive; this work

The Journey to the Journey   39

builds a stunningly sophisticated capacity in participants to look at the full complexity of their experiences, identify an issue that is personally compelling and alive, sift through all the complexity around that issue, formulate a set of questions related that issue, and then find the right question that clearly presents the essence of that issue and invites a powerful and focused discussion related to that issue. If the quality of learning at every IJ session depended on the clarity and significance of the question brought to the group by participants, then this process illuminated a path to supporting every AmeriCorps member in achieving this vital clarity as part of the preparation for every IJ session.

I'll have a lot more to say about the work of question formulation in Chapter 6 because this process has become so central to this approach to leadership development that it merits a thorough explanation. For now, I'll just say that this work proved to be transformational. With this piece of the puzzle in place, feedback about the IJ began to shift all across the network. It became increasingly rare to hear AmeriCorps members criticize IJ as an unproductive space filled with venting and negativity; now, the buzz was that these conversations were engaging, important, and meaningful. Some sites began scheduling 75 or 90 minutes for IJ – instead of the required one hour – because so many AmeriCorps members were requesting more time to stay in these discussions. Question Formulation powerfully addressed a major obstacle to successful large-scale reflection, and dramatically strengthened the IJ while building every AmeriCorps member's capacity to confront and navigate the complexities of their daily service experiences.

At this point, the puzzle was almost complete. We had a new title for the curriculum – The Idealist's Journey – that grounded this work in a powerful metaphor for a year of service and that aligned the program to the organization's founding vision. We had a sequence of reflection questions that had been refined year after year to resonate powerfully with the AmeriCorps member experience. We had an approach to inviting participants into this work that eliminated hard-core resistance to this type of development and that proved effective at engaging the vast majority of AmeriCorps members in the work of reflection. And we had a Question Formulation Technique that supported AmeriCorps members in identifying and clearly presenting questions that mattered and that evoked focused and engaging learning. Finally, this whole approach was being used and refined year after year after year through use with thousands of individuals engaged in complex and demanding service work across dozens of sites.

There was just one more piece of the puzzle to figure out to unlock the full potential of this approach. In the next chapter, we turn our attention to the story of that final piece: *The Flame.*

2

DISCOVERING THE FLAME

Designers actually can change the world for the better by making the complicated simple and finding beauty in truth. – Michael Bierut (2012)

In this chapter, we turn our attention from the development of the Idealist's Journey curriculum to a parallel and related process: The experimentation that ultimately led to a visual model that conceptualized the work of developing servant leaders through a long-term service experience in a clear and powerful way. It's called *The Flame*, and the story of its development is another important window into the work of developing servant leaders at scale.

Over the course of the effort to develop an organization-wide capacity to ignite and sustain purpose, a surprising insight emerged. We learned that the way that we framed how this reflection experience fits into the bigger picture of leadership development at City Year mattered a great deal. As you'll see, we experimented with different ways of conceptualizing our overall approach to leadership development, and it quickly became clear that the way this work was framed exerted a powerful influence on how AmeriCorps members related the Idealist's Journey experience. Was the reflection work just one among many tasks to complete in our leadership development efforts? Or was it a vital piece of inner work that influenced our ability to serve others in profound ways? We discovered that this kind of framing had a significant impact on the quality of the reflection experience across the whole organization.

We also discovered that embedded in the work of leadership development are some deep and significant questions. For example, what is the relationship between inner change (within the self) and outer change (in the world around us)? Is it optimal – or even possible – to focus on one while neglecting the other? Also, what is the relationship between organizational purpose and individual purpose? Is it enough for organizations to develop a clear purpose and then support staff in advancing that purpose? Or is there a more complex relationship between organizational and individual purpose that must be addressed?

Over the course of years of exploring ways to conceptualize the work of leadership development we found ourselves confronting these questions. In time, we arrived at answers that proved to be theoretically powerful and practically useful. We realized ultimately that inner change and outer change were, in fact, too interconnected and interdependent to separate. We discovered that organizational purpose and individual purpose are two related but distinct areas of focus. It turns out that the optimal condition is a situation in which the organization has a clear purpose, and all the people at that organization are clear about their own personal purpose . . .and see clear alignment between their personal purpose and the larger organizational purpose they spend their days advancing.

It took some time to understand all of this, and to find a way of talking and thinking about leadership development that illuminated all of this via a visual design so simple that it could instantly be understood by everyone. Once again, the story of the development of the Flame model provides vivid insight into the challenges solved by this work and the strategic contribution it makes to the effort to develop servant leaders at scale.

THE ONGOING DEBATE: SERVICE...OR LEADERSHIP DEVELOPMENT?

From the day I arrived at City Year, I encountered an ongoing debate unfolding across the entire organization focused on the following question: *Was City Year a service organization or a leadership development organization?* On the one hand, the organization existed to serve communities, and this focus on others was central to the mission of the organization. The pivot to address the high school drop-out crisis represented an audacious commitment to leverage young adults engaged in service to measurably impact a pressing public problem on a national scale. On the other hand, the organization worked with young adults and dedicated considerable time and energy to developing the service-related skills and civic leadership competencies of its AmeriCorps members. Youth development was integral to the founding vision of the organization and was vital to its mission.

To be clear, there was essentially universal agreement across the organization that the answer to this question was "Both/And": City Year was fundamentally about BOTH service AND leadership development and sought to achieve both goals in an integrated way. Yet that understanding did not seem to quiet the debate. We talked continually about how best to balance those dual commitments and referred frequently to the metaphor of a pendulum swinging toward one end and then back toward the other end from year to year. Anytime the organization became so focused on corps member development that service impact began to slip, the organization would refocus on service. And when the focus on service was so intense that corps member development had become neglected, the focus would shift back to development. This dynamic balance continued year after year, and in many ways served the organization very well.

As a student of leadership theory, however, there was something about this debate that just didn't sit right. While I agreed that City Year was about BOTH service AND leadership development, the fact that we didn't have a clear way of thinking and talking about the relationship between these two essential elements of our work was problematic. There had to be a way that these elements fit together. But how?

It's relevant to note that my six years of doctoral work were spent studying youth leadership programs, so I arrived at City Year steeped in encounters with organizations working with young people. Soon after encountering City Year, I came to the belief that it was the best youth leadership organization I had ever seen. It was amazingly effective at engaging with and developing young people and had developed an array of stunningly powerful tools, practices, and conceptual frameworks that were a testament to the energy and creativity the organization had long brought to this work.

For example, the organization had accumulated a set of practices called "Power Tools" that allowed large numbers of individuals to collaborate powerfully. One of these tools was called "Hands Up," and it was a simple but remarkably effective ritual. If any individual in a room full of City Year AmeriCorps members or staff raises their hand, everyone else quickly raises their hand and stops talking; within a matter of seconds, a loud and unfocused group would transform into a silent team that was present, focused, and actively awaiting instructions or announcements. Watching this happen in a room full of more than a 1000 people at City Year's annual summer training conference is a wonder to behold. Another example of a Power Tool is a practice known as "NOSTUESO," which is an acronym for "No One Speaks Twice Until Everyone Has Spoken Once." If an individual is dominating a conversation – or if too many individuals are sitting back and not participating – someone can request to practice NOSTUESO, and participation is instantly made more even and inclusive.

On the one hand, I found these tools and practices to be incredibly powerful and useful. When I had opportunities to connect with other organizations, I often privately lamented the absence of these tools. Watching a speaker spend a full minute trying to get a chatty audience to quiet down and focus or participating in a discussion in which one or two strong personalities dominated the discussion, I found myself wishing I could just reference a power tool like Hands Up or NOSTUESO and have everyone understand what I was talking about.

On the other hand, for all their power and value, all of these tools and practices did not represent a clear conceptual framework that illuminated City Year's approach to leadership development in a comprehensive way. As the service model grew more and more sophisticated, the lack of a clear approach to leadership development grew more problematic. It's hard to do something with excellence if you are not really clear about what you are doing.

I can remember one meeting that occurred a couple years into my tenure. It pulled together staff from multiple departments as well as an outside consultant and was scheduled for three hours, an usually long time for a meeting at the organization. The goal was to emerge with a clear framework for leadership development, and we began by reviewing all the different tools, practices, and frameworks that the organization used for this work. Should a framework known as "the leadership compass" be elevated to represent our core approach to leadership development? The power tools? Other concepts? At the end of three hours, we were unable to arrive at any clarity.

Several months after that meeting, events unfolded that led to an important breakthrough in this work. Col. Robert Gordon joined City Year as a Senior Leader around 2008; he was a former Army Ranger with years of experience at senior levels at the Pentagon who had also been deeply involved in the development of AmeriCorps and America's national service movement. Col. Gordon served as a human bridge between the worlds of military and civilian service and joined the organization with a mandate to guide our leadership development efforts. He was the individual who first introduced City Year to the US Army's simple yet profound approach to leadership development: *BE, KNOW, and DO.*

After centuries of engaging in the work of civic leadership development, the Army had arrived at this three-word phrase that distilled the complex work of leadership development to its absolute essence. The phrase presented the three approaches that were essential to the development of leaders:

1. BE: Values, Character and Integrity.

2. KNOW: Knowledge, Skills, Competencies.

3. DO: Action in the World.

These three simple words captured all the different ways that the Army sought to develop its soldiers.[1] It was exactly

---

[1] To learn more, check out Be, Know, Do: Leadership the Army Way, by Fances Hesselbein and General Eric K. Shinseki (Jossey Bass, 2004).

the sort of framework that we were lacking, and in embracing it we would be strengthening the connection between the worlds of military and civilian service. Soon after Col. Gordon's arrival at the organization, we began to present this framework to our AmeriCorps members as City Year's leadership development model.

In that first year, we shared this concept in table format, using a grid to explain what each of these words meant to our organization. We struggled a bit with how to conceptualize the power of our culture as a leadership development experience, so we added here as the overall context in which Be, Know, Do occurred. For a look at how we presented this work in its first iteration, see Fig. 1:

This was a big step forward in terms of providing a high-level overview of our approach to the work of leadership development. We quickly learned that the phrase "Be, Know, Do" was "sticky," meaning that AmeriCorps members and staff found it understandable and helpful and began using it in their day-to-day work. Still, the limitations to this approach quickly became clear.

Perhaps the best way to describe the problem here was that this approach was inelegant. It was prose-heavy and full of phrases presented in small font; this is the kind of Power Point slide that gives people headaches as they try to figure out what it all means. It also represented a clunky way to conceptualize the importance of City Year's unique culture of idealism. The culture was the result of years of creativity and effort and was one of the vital ways that the organization developed individuals; including it here as a small box of text labeled "Context" did not really do justice to the power and importance of this work.

Most significantly from my perspective, though, was the way this model influenced the way AmeriCorps members understood and engaged with the reflection work. On the

Leadership Development

The "Be, Know, Do" Framework

Pillar	BE	KNOW	DO
Key Question	Who do I want to be?	What skills do I need?	How can I effect change?
Relevant Elements of City Year Experience	Building Self-Awareness Through: 1) Service Experience Reciprocal transformation through service with communities 2) Reflection Through the Idealist's Journey	Building Civic Skills Through: 1) Professional Development Training Workshops, Personalized Coaching, and Self-directed Learning 2) Skills Assessment Performance Management Process	Building the Beloved Community Through: City Year Service Programs: 1) Whole School, Whole Child 2) Heroes Continuum 3) Civic Engagement
Context	CityYear Culture of Idealism		
Leadership Outcomes	Civic Identity (Self Concept) "I am someone who makes the community better"	Civic Capacity "I can (and have the skills and knowledge to) make the community better"	Civic Action "I lead to make the community better"

Fig. 1. Early Effort to Present the "Be, Know, Do" Leadership Development Framework to City Year AmeriCorps Members.

one hand, it was helpful to be able to say "The IJ is our effort to develop the BE." On the other hand, we heard from AmeriCorps members who said, essentially, "Yeah, I get that. But everything I have to focus on in the KNOW and DO columns is way more urgent and important. We just don't have time for that BE stuff."

This was a shift from the earliest days of the reflection work, when the majority of AmeriCorps members found it to be an unproductive space rife with negative energy and trivial conversations. We had figured out how to make the space more productive...but when compared with the other ways individuals could spend their time, it was easy to dismiss this work. When presented this way, AmeriCorps members couldn't help but assume that even if they didn't do any of the BE work, they were still doing two thirds of what we viewed as the essential work of leadership development. Given the urgency and clear impact of that two thirds that surely wasn't such a bad thing.

Intuitively, I sensed that there had to be some way of presenting all of this in a way that went beyond this prosaic three column table. Surely, there was a way of moving beyond simply presenting "Be, Know, Do" as three categories of work. What if we could represent the relationship between these elements in a way that powerfully illuminated the profound relationship between the sort of inner work done in the BE column and the impact created in the DO column? There had to be a better way, but I couldn't see what it was.

The answer came to me one day as I was walking down a hall at HQ thinking about something totally unrelated.

A Flame

Be, Know, and Do are more than just categories in a table; they are actually *nested within each other*. The movement

Fig. 2. Revised "Candle" Approach to Presenting the "Be, Know, Do" Leadership Development Model to City Year AmeriCorps Members.

from DO to KNOW to BE is a move from external to internal, and we could visually represent that relationship with a set of nested flames. In addition, whatever the flame was grounded in could represent the culture!

I ran back to my desk and created a new image (Fig. 2), which is what we used to present this work to the following year's batch of AmeriCorps members.

No more tables filled with 12-point font; no more clunky ways of thinking about the relationship between our powerful organizational culture and the individual development of each individual AmeriCorps member. The image was so simple that anyone could understand it, but it presented an elegant and sophisticated way of representing our approach to leadership development.

Once we began presenting this as our leadership development model, the feedback from AmeriCorps members began to shift in subtle but important ways. One could not respond to this framework with a belief that one could neglect the "Be" dimension of the work and still be doing 2/3rds of the work of leadership. With this image, it becomes apparent that the choice to neglect the "Be" is a choice to neglect the deepest, most personal work of leadership development. Simply being able to state the phrase "the Be level of the Flame" made it possible to talk with clarity and shared understanding about an aspect of leadership development that had previously been very difficult to discuss effectively.

Once this model was shared with the organization, the resistance to this work shifted from "There's too much other important work to be done," to "This kind of reflection is really hard for me." For many AmeriCorps members – surely those that in previous years had offered the most vocal resistance to this work – turning inwards to engage in reflection and introspection was an uncomfortable and challenging task. With the language of "invitation," they could no longer resist the work by claiming that they were being compelled to do this, and with the Flame, they could no longer dismiss it as unimportant. What was left was a recognition that this was something they found to be personally challenging. This shift may seem subtle, but it was profound. This seemingly simple visual design represented a breakthrough in the effort to find ways to help people understand the value of this work and invite a wider circle of individuals to be willing to engage with it.

Equally important, the Flame offered a powerful answer to two questions buried deep in the work of leadership development:

What is the relationship between inner change and outer change?

What is the relationship between organizational values and individual values?

As you may have noticed, the first of these questions is just a slight rephrasing of the debate that had been ongoing at the organization since its founding: *Is City Year a service organization or a leadership development organization?* The Flame allowed us to go beyond asserting that the answer is "BOTH/ AND;" we could now offer a framework for understanding the profound interconnectedness between our inner growth and development (the BE and KNOW) and our impact on the world around us (the DO). We began sharing the following graphic (Fig. 3) in our presentations introducing the Flame of Idealism:

In other words, in the very first days of the program year, the Flame challenged AmeriCorps members to operate with a consciousness that their own growth and development and their capacity to serve others were too interconnected to separate. We made it clear that we would give them opportunities to consistently turn inwards amid the demands of serving others; whether they would make the most of those opportunities was up to them. But the conceptual model made it clear right from the start that the dual processes of inner development and service impact were too interconnected to separate.

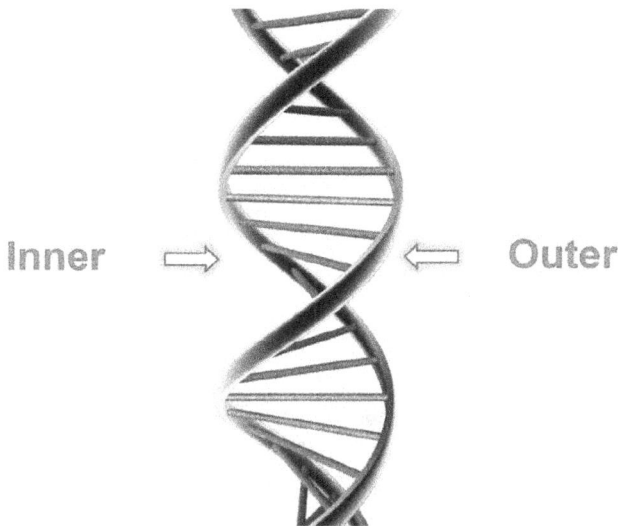

Fig. 3. DNA Image Used to Demonstrate the Interconnected Relationship of Inner and Outer Change to City Year AmeriCorps Members.

As for the second question related to the relationship between organizational values and individual values, I arrived at the following insight: This was an issue that was buried so deep in the work of leadership development that even many individuals who were highly experienced in the work of organizational design didn't recognize it as a problem. It is considered a best practice of high-performing organizations to operate with a clear and powerful set of core values. It is hardly revolutionary to state that this kind of organizational clarity is vitally important for any organization to survive and thrive amid the complexities of the world. The problem arises, though, when organizations achieve this clarity...and then assume that the next step is to simply download this clarity into all of their staff.

Employees are not simply empty buckets to be filled with organizational values; they are individuals with rich life experiences and pre-existing core values that draw them to work for particular organizations. They may not yet have done the work to fully understand those personal values, but they are in there, and it's problematic to assume that when individuals join an organization, they simply internalize the organization's values exactly as expressed by the posters on the walls around the office.

The truth is that individuals have their own core values, and individuals become high-performers and long-term employees where there is a high degree of alignment between their personal values and the organizational values. The Flame makes clear that it is optimal for the organization to have a set of clear values and for all the individuals in that organization to have clarity about their own personal core values as well. If they have this clarity and there is deep alignment between their personal values and the organizations' values, they will be intrinsically motivated to perform and contribute at the highest level. If they get clear about their personal values and realize that they are not in alignment with the organizational values, it is best for all involved for them to move on sooner rather than later. Employees without this alignment are sure to be disengaged and unmotivated, and when we focus on trying to compel employees to embrace organizational values – rather than clarify and live their own values – we actually conceal and compound this problem rather than address it productively.

Here's a quick story to illustrate the problems that arise when organizations have not grappled with the need to focus on both organizational values and individual values:

In one of my final years at City Year, a colleague of mine invited me to run a 90-minute "Leading with Purpose" training for about 25 experienced consultants employed by one of the country's major professional services firms. This firm had recently made a focus on purpose central to its brand, and its efforts to make purpose central to its culture included videos from senior leadership talking about the firm's values and the importance of purpose to the organization's mission. When I invited the participants at this session to craft their own personal mission statements, I was surprised, then, to find that they had never been asked to reflect on this. At the end of the reflection time I gave for drafting a mission, one clearly frustrated individual had not written anything in his notebook.

"I have no idea what my mission is," he said. "I've never been asked to think about this at all."

This was a highly educated, high-performing, well-compensated employee doing complex technical consulting work at a firm that was trying to make purpose central to their brand...yet he had never been asked to develop a clear personal sense of purpose. This is what it looks like when organizations don't grasp that organizational purpose and individual purpose are related but distinct.

At the end of the brief training, I asked the group this question: "What would it look like if every individual at this firm operated with a clear, powerful sense of personal mission?" The first answer offered was as follows: "We would double our billion-dollar market value." I have no idea if that statement was actually true, but the fact that it was said out loud was a testament to how meaningful this exercise felt to this room full of experienced professionals who were already immersed in an organization supposedly dedicated to purpose. This is the insight that is illuminated so clearly by the Flame: A clear organizational purpose may be essential, but that alone is not sufficient. The key to truly optimal performance is an organization with a clear purpose comprising individuals who are powerfully connected to their own uniquely individual senses of purpose.

At City Year, we learned that the seemingly simple visual image of the Flame helped us to conceptualize this relationship between individual and organizational purpose clearly. Equally important, this model led AmeriCorps members and staff to be more bought-in and engaged with the reflection work in ways that strengthened the power and effectiveness of that aspect of our leadership development work.

"THE TORCH HAS BEEN PASSED TO A NEW GENERATION. . ."

With the conceptual framework of the Flame in place, we were very, very close to having a final model of leadership development for City Year. There was still one part of the model that just didn't quite sit right with me, though. Representing the "Culture" as a partially illustrated candle felt problematic; again, the image didn't seem to honor the power and importance of organizational culture, and I felt a twinge of frustration every time I saw that image.

Once again, a better solution came to me one day while I was focused on something unrelated. Rather than representing the Flame as a candle, *what if we represented it as a torch*? With some help from our communications department, we developed the following image (Fig. 4):

This small but significant tweak took this work to an entirely new level of power and impact. The co-founders of City Year, Michael Brown and Alan Khazei, had both said many times that one of the inspirations for launching the organization was the call to service and idealism issued by President John F. Kennedy. The idea for City Year in particular and national service in general represented a very concrete and practical response to one of President Kennedy's most iconic

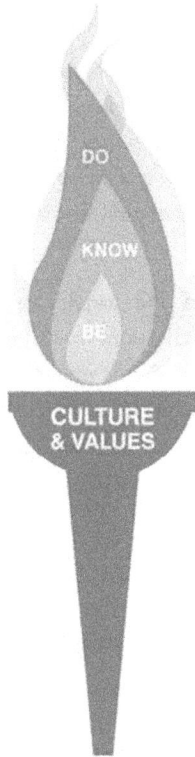

Fig. 4. Final "Torch" Approach to Presenting "Be, Know, Do" Leadership Development Model to City Year AmeriCorps Members.

challenges: "Ask not what your country can do for you; ask what you can do for your country." Kennedy also had this to say at his inaugural address on January 20th, 1961:

> *Let the word go forth from this time and place, to friend and foe alike,* that the torch has been passed to a new generations of Americans, *born in this century, tempered by war, disciplined by a hard and bitter*

*peace, proud of our ancient heritage – and unwilling
to witness or permit the slow undoing of those
human rights to which we are committed today and
around the world. Let every nation know, whether it
wishes us well or ill, that we shall pay any price, bear
any burden, meet any hardship, support any friend,
oppose any foe to assure the survival and the success
of liberty.*

With the image of the torch, we not only distilled a
sophisticated conceptual framework for leadership development into a remarkably simple image; we also grounded that
theoretical sophistication in a metaphor that evoked the
passionate commitment to idealism, service, patriotism, and
human rights that animated and inspired the entire
organization.

THE FINAL ELEMENT: INTEGRATING THE SHADOW

After years of experimentation, it felt like we had achieved our
goals. We had a model of reflection that was effective at scale,
and a conceptual framework that allowed us to talk and think
about leadership in powerful ways that integrated inner and
outer change. It turned out, though, that we needed one more
vital aspect of this work before this approach would be truly
whole and complete.

City Year's pivot to addressing the high school drop-out
crisis was audacious and inspiring. As we have already seen,
this change in focus meant that AmeriCorps members were
delivering increasingly sophisticated service in high-need
schools while driving toward measurable results to be
shared with key stakeholders like school districts and funders.
Given the increase in the demands on everyone at the

organization, it was not surprising that levels of stress and anxiety increased as the focus on impact grew ever more intense. Also, the context in which this work was happening was growing notably more turbulent and traumatic. This was the era when Black men like Eric Garner in Staten Island, Michael Brown in Ferguson and Treyvon Martin (a teenager) in Cleveland were killed, and the issue of race – always simmering in this country – erupted yet again into public consciousness. For the highly diverse City Year corps and staff working in schools filled with mostly Black and Brown children, these events hit very close to home, evoking intense feelings of anger, fear, despair, guilt, and shame.

The increase in difficult emotions was apparent in the Idealist's Journey sessions, where AmeriCorps members had the opportunity to discuss the challenges they were encountering in their experiences. The reality was that the pressures to achieve service impact were not going anywhere, and the injustices occurring all around us were painful truths that AmeriCorps members were deeply committed to confronting with honesty and courage. In the face of all of this, a new leadership development challenge emerged: Was there a way to support the organization in handling the increased stress, challenges, and difficult emotions evoked by this work and this historical moment more consciously and effectively?

After watching this pressure grow – and experiencing the increase in difficult emotions myself – I realized there was something we could try that might empower us to work with all these dark emotions with more skill, consciousness, and wisdom.

As an organization, we had to confront the shadow.

My first encounter with shadow work had occurred during a powerful personal growth experience the year before I came to City Year. As part of a weekend-long retreat, I was challenged to not only write my personal mission statement, but also to craft my "shadow mission": a related statement that clearly illuminated the choices I made when I chose not to align my actions with my espoused mission. As expected, my mission was aspirational, noble, and inspiring. By forcing myself to look at who I was being when I was not aligned with that mission, I was compelled to confront a part of myself that was ignoble, shameful, lazy, and cowardly. It wasn't pretty or pleasant, but it was painfully familiar. The shadow mission exercise illuminated a way of being that was real, honest, and excruciatingly uncomfortable to confront so directly.

The exercise had a deep impact on me, and over the years, I researched the concept of shadow in more depth. This notion is deeply informed by the work of psychologist Carl Jung, who had a lot to say about the subject. He believed that we cannot really know ourselves fully until we have confronted our own shadow; this embrace of both the light and the darkness within the self is the only path to achieving psychological and spiritual wholeness. He also asserts that when we have not confronted our shadow, our own "dark side" influences our behavior in ways that are beyond our conscious awareness; the more conscious we are of our own shadow, the more skillfully and intentionally we can choose not to act from that place. Finally, Jung believes if there are dark and undesirable parts of ourselves that we have not yet confronted and owned, we end up projecting those negative attributes onto some "other" in ways that are deeply problematic. We see hatred, or anger, or violence, or bigotry, or cowardice in the other when the truth is that these are aspects of the self that we refuse to own because they are so painful and socially unacceptable.

For all these reasons, Jung makes it clear that it is a difficult and painful journey to encounter one's own shadow, but it is an essential undertaking if one is to achieve integration, wholeness, and peace at both the individual and communal levels.

I had encountered these ideas before arriving at City Year but had gone years without trying to bring this work to the organization. In part, that was because I wasn't sure an organization so focused on idealism and positivity would embrace these ideas. Also, if I'm honest, the idea of bringing this work to all my colleagues was just plain scary. By definition, the shadow represents the parts of ourselves that we prefer to conceal from others; sharing it in this kind of public, professional context required a level of vulnerability that I wasn't sure I wanted to risk.

I will say a lot more about the shadow in Chapter 5. For now, it will suffice to say that after years of inviting AmeriCorps members to craft their personal leadership mission, we began challenging them to craft their related shadow mission. Somewhat to my surprise, the concept and the exercise evoked a sense of relief from individuals. After one of the first trainings I did on this topic, an AmeriCorps member told me this concept made her feel so seen and understood that she began to cry.

While not everyone had this kind of intense emotional reaction, the fact that some AmeriCorps members had this experience speaks to what can only be called the spiritual power of owning the shadow. By making it clear that every human being alive has a shadow, this work greatly diminishes the sense of shame that so often accompanies experiencing difficult emotions. It also breaks down the loneliness that results from this shame; rather than engaging in a solitary effort to repress or conceal the dark parts of ourselves, we can connect as a community of individuals collectively working to confront and work with shadow. Individuals immersed in a community that has embraced this work feel seen and honored with an entirely new level of wholeness.

It was scary to risk bringing this to the organization, but it was received with gratitude and – as hoped – made it possible to work with difficult emotions and dark parts of the self with more intentionality, skill, and wisdom. After a few pilot trainings, we built it into the Idealist's Journey curriculum and made this shadow work integral to our approach to leadership development.

THE PIECES FALL INTO PLACE

It took nearly seven years of innovation, failure, experimentation, careful listening to feedback, and patient organizational change efforts to get there, but we had finally arrived. We had built a capacity to engage AmeriCorps members in powerful personal reflection on a consistent basis, and we had found a way to represent the work of leadership development in a manner that contextualized this reflection work within all the other vital ways that City Year sought to develop AmeriCorps members. We had arrived at a conceptual approach to leadership development that combined profound simplicity with theoretical sophistication and deep metaphorical power. We had learned how to harness the power of Joseph Campbell's "hero's journey" framework, eliminate vocal resistance across the network, invite reflection on important but not urgent matters like personal mission and values, and had found a way to empower AmeriCorps members to find and present the most personally compelling questions embedded in their complex service experience. We had found a way to effectively invite individuals to confront their own shadow. And we had figured out how to do all of this at scale, at an organization that, as of this writing, engages more than 2,000 AmeriCorps members in demanding service at 29 sites across the nation.

As previously mentioned, City Year has a culture of rigorous attention to data collection and analysis, and every year gathered feedback from the entire corps regarding their satisfaction with the work that eventually became the Idealist's Journey. The chart is presented in Fig. 5:

The rising slope of that line is the story of the developments described in the past two chapters; it's a visual testament to the emergence of a new organizational capacity to guide individuals through a powerful process of inner development at scale.

In those final years of the program's development, AmeriCorps members reported that this experience achieved the following goals:

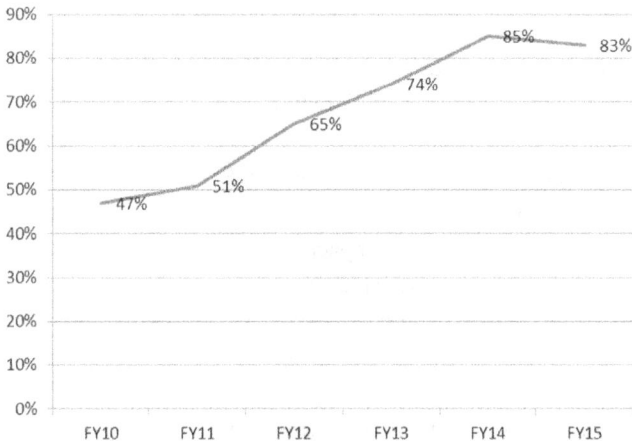

Fig. 5. Graph of Evaluation Data Showing Increase in Satisfaction With the Idealist's Journey Curriculum at City Year Over the Years 2010–2015.

- Helps me to maintain a broader perspective on my daily experiences.

- Challenges me to attain a deeper understanding of myself.

- Helps me to be more mindful and present while delivering service.

- Helps to build a stronger City Year community.

- Challenges me to think more deeply about my service.

Given the work AmeriCorps members are challenged to do every day, the organizational capacity to drive these outcomes is highly strategic.

It's important at this point to zoom out a bit and remember the larger mission this work was designed to serve. City Year has set audacious goals to make a measurable impact on the nation's high school graduation rates, and they've made some remarkable progress. According to research, schools served by City Year gained the equivalent of approximately one full month of additional English and Math learning compared to schools without City Year. The study also found that City Year helped to drive a 51% reduction in the number of students off track in English language arts and a 50% reduction in the number of students off track in mathematics (Meredith & Anderson, 2015). In other words, City Year is making measurable, significant impact on a complex and vitally important national civic challenge.

To be clear, it would be an act of inexcusable hubris to suggest that these powerful outcomes are due primarily to the reflection and leadership development work described here. Those results reflect the hard work and dedication of thousands of staff and AmeriCorps members and could only be achieved with excellence across all departments in the organization. As I made clear at the start of this chapter, the Flame and Journey work discussed here represent just one component of the massive organizational change effort City Year undertook in its pivot to focus on education, and it is vital to keep that perspective in mind when reviewing the impact that the organization is having in schools across the nation.

It does feel fair and responsible to claim the following: At City Year – as at any organization seeking to address complex public problems – leadership development is one of many priorities that contribute to overall excellence and impact in the world. The development of the Flame and Journey described here represents an effort to bring a new level of depth, comprehensiveness, conceptual clarity, and transformational potential to this particular facet of the organization's work.

POSTSCRIPT

I joined the staff at City Year in 2006 and left a decade later in 2016. As I'm writing this, it's been nearly eight years since I left the organization, and it's reasonable to ask whether or how this work has endured. The answer is illuminating for anyone seeking to develop this kind of large-scale servant leadership development system.

Although City Year continues to thrive overall as an organization, the leadership development work described here is no longer occurring in a robust and comprehensive way. There are a few sites that continue to use the Idealist's Journey curriculum because they love the work, but it's not part of every AmeriCorps member's experience as it once was. The Flame is still shared with the AmeriCorps members, but the consistent practice of providing spaces to focus on the "Be" level is not a priority in the way it was during the years described in this book.

I see a few lessons in this outcome. First, as I explained in Chapter 1, I was recruited into City Year by the head of the Research Department who thought I would be a great fit for the organization. Over the course of my decade there, I was engaged in an act of "intrapraneurship" – I was trying to bring something new and innovative to the organization from my position in middle management. Although the organization in general and my supervisors in particular gave me a great deal of support and opportunity to move this work forward, the organization was not looking for someone to do this work when it brought me on. In the context of all of the complex organizational change work required by the pivot to addressing the drop-out crisis, this work was never a top priority for the organization as a whole. The resistance and concerns that I describe in these past chapters never fully disappeared, so when this work no longer had a full-time staff member at headquarters championing it for the network, it slowly faded away.

In addition, as the chart of satisfaction levels presented here demonstrates, the work hit an upper limit of a satisfaction rating of 85% after 10 years of work. While that represented a huge improvement from the earliest years, it's a rating that is good but not great. For this work to really reach its full potential, it needs to be fully embraced as an organizational priority. You'll learn in Chapter 7 that happened at the New Politics Leadership Academy, where this work was integral to the organization's approach to leadership development right from the beginning. When implemented in that context, this work regularly receives satisfaction ratings higher than 95%.

I hope my enduring appreciation and respect for City Year has come through clearly in the past two chapters, along with my gratitude for the senior leaders who supported this work over the course of my decade working there. I was given incredible opportunities to explore and experiment, and through it all learned the lessons I've shared here. As I bring this narrative of the development of this work to a close, I'll simply note that one of those lessons is that this work is unlikely to achieve its full potential and become an enduring aspect of an organization's culture without full support and buy-in from the highest levels of the organization.

With that, we now turn our attention to each element of the Flame to go deeper in our understanding of each of these four interdependent aspects of leadership development.

3

CULTURE AND VALUES

The only thing of real importance that leaders do is to create and manage culture. If you do not manage culture, it will manage you, and you may not even be aware of the extent to which this is happening. – Edgar Schein (1985, p. 2)

Every organization has a culture, and that culture has a major impact on the experiences of the individual in that organization and, by extension, that organization's effectiveness at achieving its mission. The key question is this: Has the culture been designed and sustained with intentionality and focus to be positive and productive, or does it simply reflect the patterns and dynamics that emerged through mindless interactions unfolding over time? Positive and intentional cultures attract top talent, call forth excellence, engage employees, and contribute powerfully to success. Cultures that are unfocused (at best) or toxic (at worst) attract B or C level talent, call forth mediocrity, drive disengagement and cynicism, and make it difficult – if not impossible – for organizations to achieve their mission.

The Flame model makes clear that an intentional productive organizational culture grounded in clear and powerful values is one of the four key aspects of leadership development. Recognizing this, high performing organizations work deliberately to ensure that this organizational clarity animates and inspires all facets of the culture. A lack of clarity, or a lack of integrity between what the organization says it cares about and what it actually does, is sure to seriously undermine the overall leadership development effectiveness of the organization.

A great deal has been written about organizational culture, and the intention of this chapter is not to provide a comprehensive review of this subject. Rather, I will focus on a few key aspects of research that have informed my journey to developing this work in substantive ways over the years. The goal is to provide an accessible mix of theory and practice related to the matter of organizational culture and values and how it relates to the work of igniting purpose at work.

Here's a roadmap for what we'll cover in the pages ahead:

First, we'll explore what happens when cultures are not intentionally designed and cultivated and how those problematic cultures undermine organizational effectiveness. We'll also think about values and the role they play in clarifying organizational purpose and influencing organizational culture.

We'll then review what some recent leadership literature has to say about what makes for a powerful and high-performing culture, encountering ideas like "cult-like cultures" and "deliberately developmental organizations" along with some examples of organizations that model those practices.

Next, we'll take a turn that may feel a bit unexpected. We'll explore the issue of worldviews, encountering leadership literature describing how the Newtonian view of the clockwork universe has shaped the way we think about organizations, and how that view is currently being challenged in fundamental ways by the new science of complex systems. We'll discuss how this shift in worldviews has profound implications for the way we understand and manage organizations in general, and how these worldviews represent barriers to implementing the focus on inner development that is central to this approach to leadership development.

TALES OF CULTURES GONE WRONG

Over the course of my professional journey, I've had my share of experiences with organizations with cultures that were, to put it generously, sub-optimal. Much of my career has been in the nonprofit sector, where I have acquired a memorable education in the unique limitations, pitfalls, and pathologies of this sector.

One of my first real jobs was working on staff of an international service program. I have many fond memories of the experience and felt highly aligned with the mission of serving abroad and supporting marginalized communities, but the organizational culture was incredibly frustrating. As with many organizations in the nonprofit sector, this institution had a very big heart and lots of empathy, but not much focus on accountability and execution. We would plan a weekend program for our participants, and plans wouldn't be finalized until the last minute, details would get dropped, and we'd spent a lot of time scrambling to put out fires that surely could have been avoided with better planning and execution. I remember for a while putting in a genuine effort to elevate the game, but the experience was something like a mix of herding cats and pushing against rubber bands; people just didn't collaborate powerfully and efforts to push on the status quo proved maddeningly ineffectual. Eventually, I adjusted myself to the norms and accepted the consistent level of frustration, ineffectiveness, and minor crisis management. Things were not horrible; in general, the participants had a positive experience and the things we planned happened, but it always felt to me that we were succeeding despite our culture, not because of it.

Following that job, I returned to the states and confronted the painful truth that I really didn't know what I wanted to do with my life. As described in the introduction, I had several years of wandering in the professional wilderness, and those years ended up becoming something of a tour of problematic organizational cultures. For example, I worked at a national test preparation company that provided tutoring in standardized tests like the SATs, LSATS, and MCATs. The pay was low, a fact that grew more problematic once I got insight into how much students were paying for these classes and how much profit the company was making. There was a litany of practices and cultural norms that made me feel devalued and exploited, and I remember clearly the day that I decided that I had to leave: We got a message from management that the cost of keeping the water cooler stocked with water would be subtracted from our paychecks;

apparently, this device was viewed as a luxury that management was not willing to provide for free. I was gone within two weeks.

I have never encountered that policy before or since, and to this day – more than 20 years later – hearing the name of that company makes me think: *That's how it feels to be treated like garbage as an employee.*

I have a lot more stories to tell, and my guess is that many readers do as well. To be honest, after several of these experiences, I found myself grappling with a deep cynicism. Was it even possible to find an organization that was not ineffective and disorganized at best and hypocritical, dehumanizing, and toxic at worst? Was there such a thing as an organization with noble and ambitious goals that operated with excellence and integrity? If so, I had never encountered it.

That changed – fortunately! – when I was hired by City Year.

It was clear from my first days at City Year that this place was different. The people around me were hard working and dedicated but also joyful and fulfilled. Rather than feeling dragged down to operate at frustrating levels of ineffectiveness and inefficiency, I felt instantly challenged to step up to operate with excellence. After years of feeling devalued and manipulated, I felt consistently respected, appreciated, seen and heard. Many of my colleagues had been at City Year for 10 or more years, and I soon understood why. Being immersed in this kind of positive, productive culture that consistently called forth my best work to advance a noble cause was a form of bliss.

THE POWER OF VALUES

It was clear from day one that City Year was a values-based organization, and that grounding in values was a key reason why the organization was so high-functioning. At the time when I began working there, the organization's values were organized and expressed via a collection of Founding Stories; these were brief, idealistic sayings, quotes or stories that embodied values that were vital to the organization.

One example of a Founding Story was a quote from a speech that Robert F. Kennedy had given in 1966 while visiting Cape Town, South Africa. He said:

> *Each time a man stands up for an ideal, or acts to improve the lot of others, or strikes out against injustice, he sends forth a tiny ripple of hope, and crossing each other from a million different centers of energy and daring those ripples build a current which can sweep down the mightiest walls of oppression and resistance. (1966)*

City Year calls this story "Ripples," and it expressed the organization's belief in the transformational power of individual small acts of service to others. City Year found creative and engaging ways to make sure this story informed the thinking and animated daily life at the organization. For example, they created an organizational ritual called "Ripples and Joys" that was used to start most meetings and conference calls across the organization. This would involve taking a few minutes for participants in the meeting to share examples of ways that our work had created positive "ripples," no matter how small. In offices across the network, you might also find a "Ripples" conference room or a "Ripples" bulletin board full of inspiring notes. All of these creative efforts served to keep us energized and connected to the work while ensuring that this value of "Ripples" lived and breathed in the daily life of the organization.

During my time at City Year, I had the great honor of participating in an initiative to "refresh" the core values.

The decision to focus on addressing the high school drop-out crisis challenged the organization to bring new levels of clarity to all facets of the organization, and this included the approach to core values. While the collection of Founding Stories continued to hold a great deal of meaning across the organization, the Senior Leadership Team decided that the time was right to develop a clear, powerful set of core values to guide us into this ambitious next chapter. The result was a months-long process that engaged staff and AmeriCorps members at all levels of the organization. Over the course of dozens of intense and engaging dialogs exploring what was truly most essential and important to City Year, we ultimately emerged with the following set of 10 core values:

1. Service to a cause greater than self

2. Students first, collaboration always

3. Belief in the power of young people

4. Social justice for all

5. Level five leadership

6. Empathy

7. Inclusivity

8. Ubuntu

9. Teamwork

10. Excellence

A deeper discussion of this list is beyond the scope of this chapter, but I have included this list with all the descriptive text as Appendix 1 at the back of this book (if you are wondering what "Ubuntu" or "Level Five Leadership" mean,

I encourage you to check it out). For now, I'll just say that the intense and engaging process of getting to this list was an example of how committed City Year was to the importance of values. Once this list was rolled out, individuals across the organization began finding creative ways to keep these values alive; examples include everything from signage around the office to public recognition of staff or AmeriCorps members who embodied a value that week to "Values Band" bracelets that AmeriCorps members could hand out to students who modeled particular values during the school day.

Clearly, these core values were not just empty slogans in the employee handbook. The represented deep and authentic commitments that animated, inspired, and guided the work of everyone across the organization. To work at the organization was to live one's professional life immersed in these values in ways that shaped one's thoughts and actions in powerful and intentional ways over the course of one's tenure at the company.

Of course, many organizations lack this deep commitment to a clear set of values. Some organizations simply haven't taken the time to develop a clear set of values. Others may have a list created, but those values are lifeless words that do not actually influence daily life at the organization. Many staff may not know what values are, and they live as impotent words on a page rather than deep commitments that guide everything that happens across the organization.

In the worst cases, espoused values are a cynical façade designed to distract attention from a truly toxic culture. Consider, for example, the case of Enron, the enormous energy company that imploded in a scandal of corruption, dishonesty, arrogance, and greed. The company had taken the time to craft what it called a "Vision and Values Statement" that could be found on the walls around the Enron office. The statement claimed that the firm conducted itself according to the following four "Capital 'V' Values": *Integrity, Communication, Respect, and Excellence.* Ultimately, the company collapsed as a result of wildly unethical and dishonest business practices actively encouraged by a toxic and dysfunctional corporate culture, costing investors nearly $75 billion dollars. Among the many lessons to learn from the cautionary tale of Enron, surely one is that the consequences can be very, very severe when core values represent nothing but empty words on a plaque in the lobby.

EXPLORING THE LITERATURE RELATED TO ORGANIZATIONAL CULTURE

For me, the encounter with City Year's powerful, intentional culture evoked the saying that "the raindrop is happiest when it rejoins the river." I felt deeply at home in a culture that celebrated idealism, teamwork, and service to others, and from the day I joined I loved participating in these rituals that clearly had the desired impact of keeping me focused, positive and connected to my colleagues and our shared mission. Over time, however, I saw people join the organization who clearly didn't feel the same. To them, City Year's culture was full of happy-clappy summer camp silliness that was unprofessional and more than just a little bit weird. Those folks tended to not last very long, I noticed.

In their seminal book *Built to Last*, Jim Collins and Jerry Porrass present findings from rigorous research into "visionary companies" – businesses that have endured for long periods of time (Collins & Porras, 1994). Specifically, they looked at companies that were premier organizations in their industry, had made a major impact on the world, and were at least 50 years old. Their research included comparison

companies in the same industries that were high performing
for a while but proved unable to stand the test of time. The
research produced a series of principles – many of which were
surprising and counterintuitive – that were present at all the
visionary companies.

One of those principles focuses on the finding that a key
element of visionary companies is what Collins and Porras call
"Cult-Like Cultures." These organizations have incredibly
strong cultures with rituals, practices and norms that bring
organizational values and beliefs powerfully to life. These cultures are intense in ways that inspire and energize employees
who are a good fit for the institution while quickly alienating
individuals who aren't. If you are not deeply passionate about
customer service, you probably won't last long at Nordstroms;
if you aren't all in on making people happy, Disney is not the
place for you. And if you aren't fully committed to idealism and
service to others, City Year's culture of idealism will annoy you
within your first hours on the job.

As Collins and Porras are careful to note, it's not that these
organizations are actually cults; it's that the strength and
intensity of their cultures are "cult-like" in that they are deeply
appealing to a particular type of person while alienating
individuals who are not fully aligned with the mission and
core values of the organization. They are not generic "great
places to work" that will appeal to everyone; they are great
places to work for those who are aligned and are places of
misery for those who aren't. For those who stick around, the
culture itself develops individuals in ways that strengthen and
advance the organization in powerful and ongoing ways.

In recent years, a small but growing community of organizations have begun exploring approaches designed to
unleash the full potential of organizational culture to promote
individual development. It's a movement documented by

Harvard scholars Robert Kegan and Lisa Lahey in a book called *An Everyone Culture: Becoming a Deliberately Developmental Organization* (Kegan & Lahey, 2016). "Deliberately Developmental Organization (DDO)" is the term Kegan and Lahey created to describe a firm that makes the development of individual employees the central focus of the culture. They explain the concept as follows:

> *In ordinary organizations, most people are doing a second job that no one is paying them for. In businesses large and small; in government agencies, schools and hospitals; in for profits and in nonprofits, and in any country in the world, most people are spending time and energy covering up their weaknesses, managing other people's impressions of them. . . .hiding their inadequacies, hiding their uncertainties. Hiding their limitations. Hiding. . . . The total cost of this waste is simple to state and staggering to contemplate: It prevents organizations, and the people working in them, from achieving their full potential. . . . What is the alternative? Imagine so valuing the importance of developing people's capabilities that you design a culture that itself immersively sweeps every member of the organization into an ongoing developmental journey in the course of working every day. (2016, pp. 1–5)*

Kegan and Lahey offer several examples of companies seeking to operate as DDOs. One example is an e-commerce tech company called Next Jump, creator of the popular and profitable "perksatwork.com" platform. Individuals who want to work at Next Jump must get invited to an intense "Super Saturday" all-day hiring experience that occurs twice a year. Over the course of nine hours of programming, job candidates are rated by multiple current staffers on characteristics like humility, grit, and willingness to help others. Individuals who make it through that intense first hurdle are invited to participate in a three-week long "Personal Leadership Boot Camp" that begins with participants exploring their greatest character weaknesses. Once those weaknesses are identified, participants focus on activities and challenges they can undertake to strengthen and develop those weaknesses.

The culture at Next Jump is built around the understanding that everyone from the CEO on down has challenges and weaknesses that can be strengthened through intentional practice. Feedback is both offered and received as an expression of support, and staff are constantly given stretch assignments that give them opportunities to learn and develop in new ways. Individuals who are unwilling to be honest and open about their own limitations and areas for growth are unlikely to last long at Next Jump (if they somehow make it through the rigorous hiring process). Those who are willing to live with this kind of vulnerability and commitment to continuous personal growth find Next Jump to be a uniquely rewarding and meaningful place to work.

Another firm highlighted as a DDO is the hedge fund Bridgewater Associates, which takes its commitment to transparency and growth to surprising extremes. At Bridgewater, every meeting at every level of the organization is recorded, and the recordings are made accessible to everyone at the organization. If people not in the original meeting listen to the recordings and have questions or concerns, they are encouraged to raise their issues with those involved in the meeting. It's an expression of one of the foundational beliefs of the organization:

> *Create a culture in which it is OK to make mistakes*
> *but unacceptable not to identify, analyze, and learn*

> *from them. Do not feel bad about your mistakes or*
> *those of others. Love them! Don't worry about*
> *looking good – worry about achieving your goals.*
> *When you experience pain, remember to reflect.*
> *(Kegan & Lahey, 2016, p. 48)*

Kegan and Lahey highlight these organizations because they are outliers in terms of the degree to which a focus on individual development is made central to their organizational culture. There is, of course, an obvious and inevitable question that arises when one encounters this approach to organizational culture: *Is it good for business?* Kegan and Lahey frame the question in this way:

> *"I'm not going to call their leaders naïve, or their*
> *companies cults, as I've heard some people do," one*
> *business analyst told us, "but it's clear these folks are*
> *playing a fundamentally different game...If you*
> *want to use your business as a kind of prop to run a*
> *university or Human Potential Center...All power to*
> *you. But you better have deep pockets or a product*
> *that sells itself – some way to pay for all this fooling*
> *around – because otherwise bankruptcy is right*
> *around the corner. This may be a good way to help*
> *Jake or Jennifer find their voice, but it's no way to*
> *run a real business." (p. 163)*

As Kegan and Lahey make clear, the answer to the question of whether being a DDO is good for business is a resounding "Yes." They note that Bridgewater was recognized by *The Economist* magazine as having made more money for its investors than any other hedge fund in history, and Next Jump was highlighted by *Inc.* magazine as "the most successful company you've never heard of." (pg. 164). It turns out that the industry average for turnover of coders working at high-tech companies is around 40%; at Next Jump, annual turnover is in the single digits. If you consider the financial costs and the productivity losses involved in replacing even a single employee, the benefit of a culture that retains talent at this level – and develops that talent over time to ever greater degrees of skill and effectiveness – is immense.

For another example of business success grounded in a unique culture that emphasizes honesty, transparency, trust, and empowerment, we can look to Netflix. It's a company that has been extraordinarily successful in a financial sense: One dollar invested in the organization in 2002 would have been worth $350 in 2019; that same dollar invested in an index fund like the S&P 500 or NASDAQ over the same time frame would be worth between $3–4 (Hastings & Meyer, 2020, p. wvi). Equally important, the organization has had a massive cultural impact, producing original programming like *Orange is the New Black*, the *Queen's Gambit*, and *Stranger Things* that were hits in the United States and a host of other programs that achieved similar levels of success in nations around the world.

In recent years, Netflix has been challenged by the rapidly changing landscape of video streaming as well as the strikes by writers and actors that have convulsed the entertainment industry as a whole. Still, there is value in exploring how the organization grew so rapidly in scale and artistic influence. Those who seek to understand the secret to this kind of achievement find themselves once again encountering a now-familiar culprit: A unique, powerful, and intentionally crafted organizational culture.

The "Netflix Culture Deck" has achieved legendary status in the world of Silicon Valley and beyond. It's a 127-slide PowerPoint deck that lays out the bold approach to culture practiced by Netflix. Originally created for internal use, by Netflix founder Reed Hastings, it was made public in 2009.

It's easily accessible on the internet and has been viewed by millions. The underlying philosophy and key ideas were recently presented in more detailed form in a 2020 book called *No Rules Rules: Netflix and the Culture of Reinvention*, by Reed Hastings and Erin Meyer (2020).

The essential elements of the Netflix culture are values that by now should be starting to sound familiar. Hire talented people who are not only high performers but are also able to collaborate and willing to learn and grow. Create a culture of radical candor, in which honest feedback is both given and received with an understanding that directly and courageously addressing even difficult issues is in the best interest of both individual growth and organizational effectiveness. Then, remove controls as much as possible to empower employees to create and innovate with as few restraints as possible in a culture of "freedom and responsibility." (Hastings & Meyer, 2020, p. xx)

In many ways, Netflix's commitment to removing controls goes to lengths that many find difficult to fathom. Perhaps the best-known example is the organization's approach to vacation policy and tracking, which is, quite simply, "There is no policy or tracking." The single slide of the culture deck presenting this info goes on to say, "There is also no clothing policy at Netflix, but no one comes to work naked. Lesson: you don't need policies for everything." (Hastings & Meyer, 2020, p. xv).

In the eyes of many, this kind of freedom is reckless, irresponsible, and certain to backfire. They imagine that when confronted with this kind of "no rule rule," employees will either never take vacation – leading to bitterness and burnout – or will disappear for weeks at a time in a shameless effort to abuse this kind of freedom. The same goes for creating controls and sign-offs related to significant expenditures. At Netflix, employees are empowered to spend significant sums of money

– up to and including sums in the hundreds and even millions of dollars – without attaining written approval from supervisors. Again, this kind of freedom triggers all kinds of fears in the minds of many who are certain that employees can't be trusted with this kind of freedom, as they are sure to abuse these freedoms in ways that are detrimental to the company.

At Netflix, however, this is all part of their commitment to building a culture that balances freedom and responsibility. They understood from the start that in a creative industry like entertainment, too many processes and control drives away top talent, who can and should be trusted and empowered to do the work they were hired to do. If there are mid-level performers who are underperforming and abusing their freedoms, the response is not to introduce controls designed to put guardrails around the mid-level talent; the response is to fire anyone who needs that kind of control in order to preserve an environment in which top talent are unleashed to operate with freedom and trust (the Culture Deck explains it this way: "Adequate performance gets a generous severance package.").

Hitting the Limits of a Worldview

I invite you to pause for a moment here and reflect on your own personal reaction to these stories of organizational cultures that provide this degree of freedom, responsibility, and expectation of ongoing growth and development. Are you someone who finds all of this exciting and compelling? Are you thrilled by this degree of liberation and do you dream of working at firms like these? Or, is your response something more akin to fear? Somewhere deep down inside, you are certain that when controls are removed, chaos ensues. In your mind, the application of rules and control is not simply necessary; it is a moral imperative for anyone who seeks to protect all that we have created from the destructive forces of chaos lurking all around us. I've learned that not everyone is excited by the idea of working at a DDO that provides radical freedom and intense accountability. Resistance to this approach to the design and management of organizations can be intense.

This was a phenomenon that I found myself grappling with repeatedly over the course of this effort to build an organizational capacity to cultivate and sustain inner development. The Journey approach to developing individuals at the innermost "BE" level of the Flame is fundamentally about freedom and trust. It is grounded in the understanding that organizations can't download purpose into people; rather, we must invite them to connect with their own unique purpose and hold a space in which they can engage in that inner work. We also can't tell them what should matter most to them; rather, we can empower them to get clear about what they personally feel is most compelling about their experiences. At its essence, this work is grounded in the belief that at the deepest level, people know what they need to know and can be trusted to find their own way forward. All of this requires releasing the need to provide control.

As I pursued this effort to open up spaces that focused on inner development, again and again I encountered fear and resistance. I remember one conversation with a senior staff person in which I explained, "We are going to let people discuss what they think is most important." The concerned response was, "What if they talk about the wrong things?" The clear implications were that providing this kind of freedom and trust even for one hour every other week was risky, as our people couldn't be trusted to use their time productively in the absence of clear guidance from above. Remember, this fear was voiced in an organization that is powerfully devoted to leadership development.

Other staff repeatedly expressed fears that these spaces would surface serious grievances related to the organization that would then have to be addressed by HR staff. The assumption was that the removal of direction and control would unleash waves of anger and grievance that would be challenging to address and that would consume time and energy that would otherwise have been spent advancing the mission.

I'll be honest: In the early days of this work, I shared these concerns, as this did seem like a realistic possibility. As the months rolled by, however, the feared explosions never materialized. As this work expanded across the organization, every year we had thousands of AmeriCorps members spending hundreds of hours engaged in these Journey spaces, and we never once had a situation where a conversation in these spaces surfaced an issue that became an HR crisis.

Actually, what happened in these spaces was the exact opposite of what was feared. Rather than surface grievances and spark crises, these spaces left participants feeling respected, trusted, and listened to in positive and productive ways. Also, these spaces provided a valuable window into the experiences and perspectives of participants in ways that allowed sites to respond to concerns before they escalated into full-scale crises. The fear that these conversations would explode into chaos was actually totally misguided. Done right, these spaces actually served to surface and address issues and concerns *before* they became crises. Explosions were actually more likely to happen when people did NOT have this kind of space to explore what was most alive for them.

To my surprise, though, staff across the network continued to voice this fear that freedom would lead to chaos and crisis even after this work had been in use at City Year for years. No matter how much evidence accumulated that people could be trusted to have these discussions, the fear that the removal of direction and control would lead to some form of chaos endured in the minds of staff. In the early years, I remember simply feeling relieved that these concerns did not come true. Over time, though, I began to question the deep assumptions that led to these fears. Where did this certainty that the removal of control would lead to chaos come from? My curiosity grew deeper as I had chances to share this work with other organizations in different contexts. I learned that these concerns were most definitely not unique to City Year; everywhere I went, this work evoked similar fears. It seemed to be an assumption buried so deep in the way people think about the world that it was simply assumed to be true: *If you remove direction and control, the world will disintegrate into chaos.*

Eventually, I arrived at an understanding of what was going on. It may feel like a detour into abstract philosophy, but I came to realize that this line of inquiry had direct and concrete implications for this effort to develop servant leaders at scale. Until these deeper assumptions are surfaced and addressed directly, resistance to this work will endure no matter how long the work unfolds free of chaos or crises.

It turns out that this belief that the universe around us cannot be trusted, that it is perpetually at risk of falling into disorder without our active and ongoing efforts to provide control, is actually embedded in a scientific worldview that has shaped our understanding of the cosmos for centuries. It's a worldview that served us well for centuries, but in recent decades, it has proven to be limited and incomplete. There is a new scientific worldview emerging that offers a dramatically different vision of how the universe works, and it has profound implications for the ways that we design and lead organizations in this world of increasing interconnection and interdependence.

One of the first individuals to explore the emergence of this new scientific worldview and what it means for our understanding of organizations is Margaret Wheatley, the author of a seminal book entitled *Leadership and the New Science: Discovering Order in a Chaotic World* (Wheatley, 2006). Wheatley notes that for the last 350 years, our understanding of the natural world has been shaped by the findings of Sir Isaac Newton, whose landmark book *Principia* was first published in 1687. With his insights about the workings of gravity, the orderly way the planets orbit the sun, and his laws of thermodynamics, he illuminated a clockwork universe that revealed the mathematical laws behind once-mysterious phenomena. Wheatley states:

> *The universe that Sir Isaac Newton described was a seductive place. As the great clock ticked, we grew smart and designed the age of machines. As the pendulum swung with perfect periodicity, it prodded us on to new discoveries. As the Earth circled the sun (just like clockwork), we grew assured of the role of determinism and prediction. (p. 28)*

The power and value of these insights was undeniable, and this understanding of the natural world came to shape the way we understand and lead organizations. Wheatley explains:

> *It is interesting to note just how Newtonian most organizations are. The machinery imagery of the cosmos was translated into organizations as an emphasis on material structure and multiple parts. Responsibilities have been organized into functions. People have been organized into role. Page after page of organizational charts depict the workings of the machine: the number of pieces, what fits where, who the most important pieces are. (p. 29)*

The problem, though, is that the science of the last century has begun to challenge this Newtonian worldview in fundamental ways. It's not that Newton is outright wrong; it is that his insights are increasingly understood to be incomplete and limited. Our studies of the natural world have revealed phenomena and dynamics that diverge dramatically from the assumptions of the Newtonian worldview. For example, Newton's third law of thermodynamics declares that for every action, there is an equal and opposite reaction. In other words, small actions generate small reactions; large actions generate large reactions. It's a law…except it isn't. The modern sciences of chaos and complexity theory have revealed the dynamic of "non-linearity," in which seemingly small actions can trigger massive reactions (consider, for example, the fact that the massive uprisings of the Arab Spring were triggered by the self-immolation of an obscure fruit seller in Tunisia).

Consider, too, Newton's second law of thermodynamics: Entropy always increases with time. Entropy is a scientific term for disorder, and the assertion here is that all around us, the natural world is forever falling into disarray and chaos. Our houses are falling apart; our cars are turning to rust; our bodies are decaying, our cities ever so slowly crumbling. Of course, entropy can be reversed or resisted by adding energy to a system. We can repaint our houses and clean our cars, exercise our bodies and rebuild our cities. But without that kind of infusion of energy, we can trust that the natural world is ever devolving into chaos.

Given this understanding of how the universe works, it is easy to understand the fears around removing processes and controls from our organizations. If direction and control represent the bulwark that separates order from chaos, only a fool or a nihilist would dare to let go of the effort to provide that direction and control.

As Wheatley explains, though, even the Second Law has its limits. She states:

> *The Second Law of Thermodynamics applies only to isolated or closed systems – to machines, for example. The most obvious exception to this law is life. Everything alive is an open system that engages with its environment and continues to grow and evolve. Yet both our science and culture have been profoundly affected by the images of degeneration contained in classical thermodynamics. When we see decay as inevitable, or society as going to ruin, or time as the road to inexorable death, we are unintentional celebrants of the Second Law. (p. 77)*

In other words, living systems are not perpetually in a process of descending into chaos; they are continually engaged in vibrant and dynamic processes of learning, growth, evolution, renewal, and self-organization. Nature is full of examples in which order, pattern, and creativity emerges in the absence of top-down authority. One classic example of how this works is the phenomenon of flocks of birds and schools of fish that swoop and turn with almost magical synchronization without a "leader" telling everyone what to do; simply by having each animal stay close to its peers an amazing level of order and creativity emerges from a collection of individual actions. All around us, we see a wild diversity of plants and flowers adapted to different environments, as well as a stunning array of animals surviving and thriving in different niches in ecosystems around the world.

The world abounds with vibrant human cultures that have emerged over thousands of years of history, and every day innovators and entrepreneurs are finding new ways to respond to current challenges and seize new opportunities. Once you know what to look for, we discover a natural world that abounds with endless order, change, creativity, and dynamism all occurring in the absence of top-down direction and control.

Wheatley states:

> *The more I read about self-organizing systems, the more I marvel at the images of freedom and possibility they evoke. This is a world of independence and interdependence, or processes that resolve so many of the dualisms we created in thought. The seeming paradoxes of order and freedom, of being and becoming, whirl into a new image that is very ancient – the unifying spiral dance of creation. State, balance, equilibrium, these are temporary states. What endures is process – dynamic, adaptive, creative. (pp. 89–90)*

In her exploration of the implications of these latest insights from science, Wheatley illuminates the assumption behind much of the fear and resistance to efforts to develop individuals at the innermost "BE" level of the Flame. Rather than living in perpetual fear of a natural world that is forever disintegrating into chaos, we can trust in a natural world that is eternally growing, evolving, learning, and adapting in endlessly creative ways.

When we apply this insight to the workings of an organization, we are challenged to live by the following creed: *People can be trusted.* They can be trusted to learn, grow and evolve. They can be trusted to innovate. They can be trusted to engage with complex situations and find their way forward. From this perspective, the constant focus on providing direction and control is not holding the forces of chaos at bay; it is squashing the creative energies of life that are seeking full expression in all of us.

Most importantly for our purposes here, it's important to highlight that these are not just esoteric philosophical musings. As we've seen, the work of creating an organizational capacity to guide individuals through inner development is fundamentally about creating spaces that allow for freedom, growth, inquiry, and exploration. Organizations that operate in an unexamined way from the Newtonian worldview will simply not be able to host and sustain these spaces. These organizations will doubt that this approach is possible, and even after seeing it work will continue to resist the approach in ways that make it challenging to sustain. This is not because the spaces are actually reckless or dangerous; it's because the organizations are operating from a worldview that relates to organizations as machines rather than living systems.

Final Thoughts

There is a well-known aphorism in the business world that "Culture eats strategy for breakfast" (this quote is often mistakenly attributed to Peter Drucker, but there is no evidence he actually said this; nevertheless, it has become a widely-accepted nugget of wisdom). The visual image of the Flame model is designed to honor this wisdom. The Flame of individual development happens in the context of the torch handle of organizational culture. That culture matters a great deal, as being immersed in any organizational culture is a developmental experience – for better or for worse.

At this point in my own journey, I have come to believe that designing a powerful and scalable approach to developing servant leaders is – relatively speaking – the easy part. Finding or developing an organization that has a culture that embraces the deeper assumptions that inform this work is actually much harder. The belief that the removal of direction and control will unleash chaos is never something that is explicitly stated and interrogated; it is a deep assumption about how the world works that informs organizational culture in very direct and concrete ways. Illuminating and then transforming these assumptions is some deep work that must be done for an organization to effectively implement this approach to developing servant leaders at scale.

In the introduction to this book I noted that the work of developing servant leaders at scale includes but transcends the work of developing leaders through one-on-one coaching or small group leadership workshops. This exploration of culture illuminates the new and distinct challenges that appear when seeking to do this kind of work at scale. If you hold the unexamined assumption that the removal of direction and control will lead to chaos, then you are sure to be skeptical – perhaps even a bit fearful – of a space that consistently invites hundreds or thousands of people to discuss what they believe is most worthy of their attention. If you assume that leadership involves telling people what to do and having answers to their questions, then you will resist opening up spaces that allow individuals to surface questions rather than download information.

This work will not endure – never mind thrive – in an organization that operates with a strictly Newtonian worldview. Until an organization fully embraces and embodies the deep assumptions that living systems can be trusted to evolve, develop, and learn in creative ways, it will not be able to open up spaces that invite individuals to develop these inner capacities powerfully and at scale. In my experience, getting organizations to even begin to recognize that they hold these assumptions is a profound challenge; guiding an organization through a journey of embracing different assumptions is the kind of work that is required if they aspire to develop servant leaders at scale.

4

DO AND KNOW

Well done is better than well said. – Benjamin Franklin (1758)

I'll begin this chapter with an assertion and a confession.

First, the assertion: Doing the right things, with excellence, is essential to achieving any goal. High performing individuals and high performing organizations do not only take action, they take effective action. Equally important, they recognize that whatever they DO is powerfully influenced by what they KNOW, so they are always engaged in learning that builds new knowledge and skills that support continual improvement. Quite simply, we create impact in the world through what we DO, and everything we DO is deeply influenced by what we KNOW.

And now the confession: This is going to be a relatively short chapter for three reasons.

First, different organizations do different work in the world, and these elements of the Flame model are the parts that relate to the very specific job-related expertise that each of us need to master in whatever work we are doing. This approach honors the vital importance of the DO and KNOW aspects of leadership development, but can only speak in very general, high-level terms about these aspects, as they differ so dramatically across different organizations.

Second, I have found that most organizations already operate with an intense focus on these elements of The Flame. From designing job responsibilities to managing performance to providing training and development, these are the aspects of leadership development that most organizations already emphasize. In fact, I have encountered many organizations that operate in ways that make it clear that these two aspects of the Flame represent the sum total of their approach to leadership development. I honor all the effort and focus already going into these areas of development, and the message I hope to send with this book is this: *Keep it going. . .and complement*

*your historic focus on DO and KNOW with a renewed focus
on the CULTURE & VALUES and the BE to provide a truly
comprehensive and holistic leadership development experience at your organization.*

And finally, there is a whole world of books and research,
skilled professionals, and consulting firms for whom this is
their core area of expertise. If you want to improve your game
in the DO and KNOW aspects of your work, there are plenty
of resources available. Because there are many other sources
of wisdom on these topics, I'll offer some general thoughts
while recognizing that deep expertise can be found elsewhere.

With all that in mind, let's dive in.

DO AND KNOW AT CITY YEAR

As discussed in Chapter 1, my time at City Year coincided
with the organization's pivot to focusing on the high school
drop-out crisis. This was a major shift in focus that required
the organization to develop a whole new area of expertise and
set of skills, with very clear and concrete implications for the
work done by the AmeriCorps members delivering service in
high-needs schools. Essentially, AmeriCorps members were
focused on improving student literacy and math skills without
having completed a master's degree in education. This kind of
service required a new level of sophistication in the knowledge
and skills that AmeriCorps members needed to be successful.

As City Year shifted to this new, more rigorous academic
focus, the organization began hiring staff and working with
consultants with deep expertise in education and academic
support. These were often individuals with doctorates in
education and decades of experience in the classroom, who
could ensure that AmeriCorps members understood the most

effective ways to build student skills in English language arts
and in math. Equally important, these skilled and knowl-
edgeable staff helped City Year to develop and provide
training to ensure AmeriCorps members had the skills and
knowledge required to do this work effectively, and the
organization developed management practices to support
AmeriCorps members in continually improving their ability to
support the success of the students that they served.

This kind of rigorous attention to doing the right work – and
having the skills and knowledge required to perform with
excellence – is vital. I watched with amazement as AmeriCorps
members shifted from relatively simple efforts like reading along
with kids to developing sophisticated understandings of specific
skills like how to build phonemic awareness or how to work
skillfully with math anxiety. This rigorous focus on developing
more sophisticated skills that allows them to take more effective
action was essential for strengthening impact.

Of course, there was a lot more going on at City Year than just
the work of AmeriCorps members. As with every organization,
professionals in different departments had to do very different
work, involving a different set of skills and knowledge. Senior
leaders were making strategic decisions for the overall organization; development professionals were raising money; IT staff
were making sure all the computers, networks and other technology were performing smoothly, and facilities staff were busy
keeping all the offices clean and functional.

I'm sure you get the point here. Every organization includes
staff focusing on different aspects of the work required to achieve
the mission, and each of those folks must DO and KNOW very
different things. Whatever those various work streams are in
your organization, there are surely a wealth of resources available to keep you informed of best practices, deepen your skills
and knowledge, and help you design roles and responsibilities in
ways that optimize the impact of your efforts. While a complete

review of all these areas of expertise is impossible, I'm happy to offer a few high-level thoughts about developing individuals at the DO and KNOW levels of the Flame.

THE 70/20/10 MODEL

Back in the 1980s, researchers at the Center for Creative Leadership in Greensboro, North Carolina were seeking to understand how to design an optimal development experience for successful managers. The result of that research was a model that has become widely known in the organizational training world.

The 70/20/10 model refers to the percentage of learning that happens in different contexts. It suggests that the optimal leadership development experiences align with the following ratio:

- 70% challenging experiences and assignments.

- 20% developmental relationships (mentoring, coaching, peer learning).

- 10 % coursework and training (Center for Creative Leadership, 2020).

The key idea here is that when it comes to our work lives, the majority of learning happens through what we would call the DO element of the Flame. The model was initially received with surprise by the academic community, who are inclined to think about learning as something that happens in a classroom or formal education experience, but this research highlights the problem of thinking about learning through that limited frame. The 70/20/10 model makes it clear that we are developed in powerful ways when we are taking action, moving things forward, and executing on our goals.

It's important to note, however, that meaningful development through experience is not guaranteed. It's possible for people to be given responsibilities that are not challenging and are solidly in their existing comfort zone. These experiences can leave people stagnant at best, or bored and actively disengaged at worst. It's also possible to give people responsibilities far beyond their capabilities, leaving them feeling overwhelmed and defeated.

Organizations that want to make the most of experience as an avenue of development must make sure that work is continually challenging. This might involve stretch assignments that have staff working right at the edge of their current skills and abilities or new experiences like working on a cross-functional team or advancing a new initiative in creative ways. In a theme that is now familiar from the previous chapter, these efforts are enhanced when they are part of an experience-driven development culture. This means that staff are recruited and hired for their openness to working at their edge, the organization knows how to create developmental challenges and support staff in taking them on, and these kinds of risks and challenges are rewarded and celebrated. The Flame and Journey approach represents a commitment to that kind of developmental experience within an organization.

JOB CRAFTING

Another approach to unlocking the full developmental potential of experience is *job crafting*. This involves changing a job to make it more engaging and meaningful, and it's an approach that has been studied for years by Yale Business

School professors Jane E. Dutton and Amy Wrzesniewski (Dutton & Wrzesniewski, 2020). They have identified three different forms that job crafting can take:

Task crafting involves altering the sequence, type or scope of tasks that comprise a job. *Relationally crafting* a job involves shifting who you interact with as part of your regular routines. Finally, *cognitive crafting* involves changing the way you interpret and make meaning of the work you are doing.

In their early research on this topic, Dutton and Wrzensnieweki interviewed sanitation staff at a hospital to ask them about their work. When asked what they did for work, some of these individuals repeated the basic responsibilities from their job description and reported that work was menial, technical, and a way to pay the bills. Others, however, reported that they found the work to be deeply meaningful and felt that they played a key role in ensuring that patients felt cared for and doctors felt supported in their work. They viewed activities like chatting pleasantly with patients and keeping rooms bright and cheerful as contributions that directly advanced the healing mission of the hospital (2001, p. 190). The research study demonstrates that two individuals doing what looks to be exactly the same work can approach their jobs in completely different ways, undertaking different tasks, engaging in different relationships, and making sense of their role and contribution to the world in radically divergent ways.

The key idea here is that experience – the DO – matters, and there are ways to unleash the full developmental potential of this element of the Flame. From taking on stretch assignments to connecting with the deeper meaning and purpose of work, it's possible to make the work we do every day a source of learning and growth.

Thoughts on the KNOW: A Word About Competencies

As we've discussed, the possibilities of what individuals DO in their work is vast, and every type of work has its own knowledge base and skill set. Once again, we can emphasize that knowledge, education, and training are vital aspects of leadership development and have an enormous influence on the effectiveness of any work we may do while recognizing that the general subject of work-related knowledge is far too vast to cover in this book. There is, however, one element of the approach many organizations take to develop staff at this level of the Flame that merits a brief discussion: Competencies.

Competencies are defined as "something you need to be able to do well in a specific job role" (Lasse, 2015). An article on the Association of Training and Development website offers the following background:

> *The term "competence" came into vogue following R.W. White's 1959 Psychological Review article, "Motivation Reconsidered: The Concept of Competence." White explains that because people are intrinsically motivated to achieve competence, having competency models enables organizations to tap into our own desire to achieve proficiency.*
>
> (Lasse, 2015)

Competencies are often broken down into "tasks," and the most fully developed models offer examples of what it looks like to perform those tasks at different levels of proficiency, usually ranging from "Beginner" or "Basic" to "Advanced."

A search for "Competencies" on Google yields list after list: "The 7 Competencies," "The 5 Key Competencies," "The 12 Leadership Competencies," "The 62 Most Common Competencies." Double click on these and another level of complexity appears, with references appearing to "threshold competencies," "functional competencies," and "management competencies." Search the term on Amazon and you'll find a small library's worth of books designed to help organizations work effectively with competencies.

On the one hand, there is surely value in bringing clarity to the skills required to be effective at a particular job. Developing a set of competencies challenges an organization to think deeply about the nature of the work they are asking individuals to undertake, and when used with skill, a clear competency model can help managers guide staff development while providing staff with useful insight into strengths and weaknesses.

On the other hand, when it comes to leadership development there are some significant limitations to what competencies can achieve.

Over the course of its evolution, City Year had put an immense amount of time and effort into developing a competency model to support AmeriCorps member development. When I started working there, City Year had a list of six Civic Leadership Competencies that it had been using for years:

1. Team Leadership.

2. Project Planning and Management.

3. Communication.

4. Working with Children and Youth.

5. Community Assessment.

6. Civic Knowledge and Imagination.

As the organization shifted to working in schools, we put an immense amount of time and energy adding details to these competencies in an effort to make them relevant to our work. We added general descriptions of each competency, a subset of skills related to that competency, and then – in an effort to make this as useful as possible as a management tool – we added a set of specific activities AmeriCorps members could undertake to demonstrate proficiency at five different levels. See Fig. 6 for an image of the "Team Leadership" Competency that was part of the AmeriCorps member management process in those days:

Team Leadership
WSWC Corps Member Version

Teamwork is one of City Year's core values and your service year is a head-first dive into the power of a team. You will learn first-hand your strengths and areas of growth as a team member when you are charged with accomplishing your service goals together. And being an effective and contributing team member helps set the groundwork for being an effective team leader – both skills you will continue to polish throughout your life as an agent of social change!

1) Increased ability to be an effective and contributing team member
By the end of the year you will be able to:
* Exercise respectful, responsive and participatory communication within a diverse team.
* Display the attitude and behaviors that foster a sense of team cohesion and help to build healthy working relationships amongst team members, including initiating and participating in proactive problem solving.
* Contribute equal effort in completing collective goals and meeting responsibilities on time to the best of your ability
* Take on increasingly demanding leadership roles within the team and support and encourage others as they take on roles that challenge their skill level within a team setting.

2) Increased ability to effectively lead a diverse team
By the end of the year you will be able to:
* Effectively facilitate team exercises and activities that encourage inclusive participation and meaningful contribution from diverse team members
* Apply situational leadership practices in reacting and responding to team needs by adapting the leadership approach to meet team needs at any given time.
* Delegate responsibilities to team members and demonstrate an ability to effectively support team members to successfully complete assigned responsibilities.
* Demonstrate an increased ability to effectively respond to and proactively manage conflict amongst team members.

Technical Challenge: Suggested Activities You Can Undertake to Demonstrate Your Skill:

Level 1	☐ Consistently meets all City Year attendance and standard expectations ☐ Read WSWC Field Guide ☐ Lead Starfish Corps team of students ☐ Demonstrates consistent use of effective communication with teammates ☐ Demonstrates the ability and willingness to be self-reflective and self-evaluative
Level 2	☐ Facilitate a team brainstorming session or debrief of an event ☐ Lead a team meeting ☐ Solicit feedback from teammates, supervisors, service partners ☐ Plan and lead team in a Starfish Corps activity/ project
Level 3	☐ Take a monthly leadership role (leading planning times/daily circles. PMOM) ☐ Serve as a PC for an internal service day or internal CY event ☐ Lead a team in a site service project or WSWC event (ex: school food drive) ☐ Lead planning of team day including logistics and team building elements ☐ Plan and lead team in implementing a Starfish Corps unit
Level 4	☐ Become a YH or CH Team Leader ☐ Help to plan an LDD including logistics and programmatic elements ☐ Develop and plan WSWC event, Starfish Corps graduation ☐ (create your own)...
Level 5	☐ Become a leader/coordinator for a City Year site wide event or program ☐ Serve as Director of Spring Camps ☐ Creates a comprehensive Legacy Plan for subsequent teams serving at site ☐ (create your own)...

Fig. 6. Rubric for "Team Leadership" Competency as It Appeared in City Year AmeriCorps Member Performance Management Document Circa 2010.

This is just one of the six competencies we developed to this level of detail. If you find yourself a bit overwhelmed by this document, you are not alone. This effort to provide AmeriCorps members with clarity and guidance was well-intentioned, but our intense focus on competencies led to a level of detail that was overwhelming to both AmeriCorps members and the managers tasked with using this rubric to provide feedback and oversight. The work of developing these rubrics, supporting managers in understanding them, and having managers review every corps member based on these rubrics consumed vast amounts of organizational time and capacity.

At some point during my time at City Year, the organization engaged the professional services firm Deloitte in a consulting engagement that included a focus on updating our AmeriCorps member management process. Deloitte had a competency list that it considered to be a best practice from the business world and encouraged us to adopt that list with some modifications to make sure it aligned with our school-based service model. We emerged from that process with the following list:

- Relationship Development.

- Team Collaboration and Leadership.

- Communication.

- Executes to Results.

- Problem-Solving and Decision-Making.

- Civic Knowledge and Fluency in Education Practice and Reform.

This time, we provided descriptions of what it looked like to demonstrate each competency at different levels of proficiency. See Fig. 7 for an image of what this approach looked like:

As you can see, this version of the competency model still includes a whole lot of detail but was surely a bit less cumbersome and overwhelming than the model that it replaced. Years later, when I made the jump to the New Politics Leadership Academy, we started off using this list of six competencies while adapting the descriptions of proficiency levels to align more clearly with the work of our organization.

That competency list lasted a couple years, until we encountered a 2015 article from the Harvard Business Review detailing how Deloitte itself had decided to completely revise its approach to performance management and embraced a new model that eliminated competencies altogether. According to authors Marcus Buckingham and Ashley Goodall, Deloitte decided to rethink its approach for several reasons (Buckingham & Goodall, 2015).

First, they recognized what we had experienced ourselves at City Year: This kind of competency-based approach to performance management consumed immense amounts of time for the organization. From completing the forms to having meetings with direct reports to discussing final ratings, the authors calculated that the organization of 65,000 employees spent more than two million hours a year on this work.

At the same time, the authors encountered a growing body of research exploring the effectiveness – actually the ineffectiveness – of manager ratings using competencies. They cite an article from the *Journal of Applied Psychology* that used a rigorous research methodology and found that 62% of the variance in manager ratings was the result of idiosyncrasies in managers perceptions; only 21% of the variance was

Competency Description and Level Guidance

Relationship Development: *Builds trust in critical partner relationships (internal and external to City Year); Demonstrates personal presence and confidence when working with partners*

BASIC: Able to connect to and related to others; Demonstrates openness, approachability, and understanding of other perspectives; maintains and builds relationships by recognizing and responding to the needs of others

PROFICIENT: Establishes and builds diverse, mutually beneficial, and sustainable partnership within City Year, throughout partner organizations, and in the communities we serve. Invests in relationships that may not address an immediate issue but further long-term objectives; balances delivery of results with relationship building.

ADVANCED: Strategically directs critical relationships to advance City Year's mission. Enables and supports City Year members and partners in their efforts to build strategic relationships by making connections and removing obstacles.

Team Collaboration & Leadership: *Collaborates with others for results; Values individual perspectives and encourages sharing of information and ideas; Provides inspirational leadership that mobilizes diverse groups towards achieving goals; Resolves team conflict in a constructive way*

BASIC: Demonstrates respect for diverse perspectives and individual strengths of team members. Actively shares knowledge, information, and ideas

PROFICIENT: Leverages diverse strengths of team members to achieve desired results; Coaches and empowers others to lead. Addresses and resolves team conflict swiftly and effectively.

ADVANCED: Builds systems and structures to facilitate collaboration and teamwork across the organization. Inspires and mobilized City Year communities to accomplish more than they thought was possible.

Fig. 7. Rubric for "Relationship Development" Competency as It Appeared in City Year Performance Management Document Circa 2014.

explained by actual differences in performance. In other words, while people assume that ratings represent some accurate assessment of performance, they are actually reflections of the individual perceptions and tendencies of the rater (Scullen et al., 2000).

To be clear, the argument here is not that a focus on developing specific competencies should be completely eliminated. I'm highlighting that the research study suggests that we should hold this element of professional development a bit more lightly. Assessing effectiveness at work is a notoriously complex and imperfect undertaking, and the effort to break it all down into a list of clear skills supported by specific tasks can provide a sense of rigor, professionalism, and effectiveness. It's a bit like reductionism in physics; it's very satisfying to identify ever smaller components of the universe, from atoms to electrons to quarks and muons. But at some point, you have to realize that you've become so focused on the parts that you've lost sight of the whole. And it's not just the folks at Deloitte who have begun to realize that this is the case.

DO AND KNOW: NECESSARY, BUT NOT SUFFICIENT

Several years ago, the Center for Creative Leadership released an influential white paper called *Future Trends in Leadership Development*, by Nick Petrie (2011). The paper presents the findings of a rigorous research project in which Petrie spoke with both leading academics in the field of leadership development and practitioners overseeing leadership development efforts at prominent organizations like Google, General Electric, and Goldman Sachs. The findings from the research effort boiled down to some insights that resonate with this Flame and Journey approach in unmistakable ways.

Petrie says:

- The environment in which work happens is becoming ever more complex.

- The skills needed to lead effectively in this environment have changed.

- Despite these trends, the methods used to develop leaders have not meaningfully changed in many years (2011, p. 6).

Petrie asked the following question to this group of scholars and practitioners: *What do you think needs to be stopped or phased out from the way leadership development is currently done?*

The responses struck a clear theme:

> *Competencies: they become either overwhelming in number or incredibly generic. If you have nothing in place they are O.K., but their use nearly always comes to a bad end.*

> *Competencies – they don't add value.*

> *Competency models as the sole method for developing people. It is only one aspect and their application has been done to death.*

> *Competencies, especially for developing senior leaders. They are probably still OK for newer managers.*

> *Static individual competencies. We are better to think about meta competencies such as learning agility and self-awareness. (2011, p. 11)*

Petrie states that the first thing to be done by organizations that want to develop leaders able to handle the growing complexity all around us is to increase their focus on "vertical" development. That type of development stands in contrast to "horizontal" development...and as you'll see, it evokes themes and concepts we've already encountered. Petrie explains this as follows:

> *Horizontal development is the development of new skills, abilities, and behaviors. It is technical learning. Horizontal development is most useful when a problem is clearly defined and there are known techniques for solving it. Surgery training is an example of horizontal development.... Vertical development, in contrast, refers to the "stages' that people progress through in how they "make sense" of their world.... In metaphorical terms, horizontal development is like pouring water into an empty glass. The vessel fills up with new content (you learn more leadership techniques). In contrast, vertical development aims to expand the glass itself. Not only does the glass have increased capacity to take in more content, the structure of the vessel itself has been transformed (the manager's mind grows bigger). (2011, pp. 11–12)*

The idea here is that technical skills and competencies are important, but any approach to leadership development that focuses solely on building those skills and competencies is sure to be limited and inadequate. Individuals don't just need new skills and information; they need to develop toward higher stages of development that allows them to hold, manage, and make sense of the world in increasingly complex ways.

How does that development happen? Again, we encounter themes that should sound familiar. It turns out that "horizontal development can be learned (from an expert), while vertical development must be earned (for yourself)" (Petrie, 2011, p. 19).

This means that organizations must learn how to consistently and effectively create spaces in which staff encounter different perspectives and new ways of thinking that challenge their assumptions and ways of making sense of the world. As a result of this encounter with complexity, they engage in an inner struggle to find ways to be with, hold, and understand these multiple perspectives. Over time, individuals engaged in this internal work have the potential to earn a "bigger mind" that allows them to hold complexity in a different way.

In other words, the latest thinking and research from the field of leadership development lends support to a key theme of the Flame and Journey approach presented here: DO and KNOW are essential aspects of developing leaders in today's world...but on their own they are limited and insufficient. There is a type of development that goes beyond gaining new knowledge and attaining new technical skills. There is another kind of development that only occurs when we hold spaces in which individuals engage with new perspectives, surface and question assumptions, and grapple in personal and meaningful ways with the complexity that they are encountering in their work and lives. Organizations that aspire to address the complex challenges of our day need to build a capacity to create these kinds of spaces powerfully and at scale. The relevance to the work of developing servant leaders at scale could hardly be more clear.

THE EXPERIENCE OF VERTICAL DEVELOPMENT: STEPPING OFF THE EDGE OF OUR KNOWN WORLD

Thus far, we've been talking about the work of leadership development with clinical terms like "vertical development" and "earning a bigger mind." As with any professional nomenclature, these terms allow us to talk about abstract concepts with some precision and shared understanding. It's important, though, to not lose sight of what it actually feels like to undertake this kind of learning journey.

Vertical development goes beyond internalizing relevant knowledge or becoming proficient in specific skills. It is about engaging in dialogue and inquiry that leads us to interrogate the perspectives and assumptions that govern our lives. As we continue to walk this path, we inevitably find ourselves in a place of confusion and disorientation, as we find ourselves beginning to question ways of thinking and relating to the world that were once comfortable and familiar. In a meaningful sense, we find ourselves moving toward the edges of the world that we know well…and then taking a step beyond, into a strange and unknown place.

At some point on the journey, we are likely to feel fear and anxiety, as those are fully appropriate responses to the journey into the unknown. We find ourselves challenged to loosen our grip on fervently held beliefs and deep assumptions while moving into a space where it's not at all clear what might replace them. As we continue on the journey of questioning the ways we have long made sense of the world, we are likely to experience strained relationships with close friends and family who are not on the same journey, making questions about who I am and where I belong both real and urgent. This kind of growth is inevitably a result of and a response to any journey into the unknown, and it is an act of courage for all those who undertake it.

It might feel a bit jarring to talk in these terms about experiences unfolding in the workplace, but if we are to understand the true nature of the type of development that we are talking about here, then we must honor the depth of the experience we are asking people to move through. Illuminating that inner journey in all its fullness is the focus of our next chapter.

5

BE

The line dividing good and evil cuts through the heart of every human being. – Aleksandr Solzhenitsyn (2007)

How are you being as you walk your path?

It's a question that invites us to reflect on aspects of the self that are so immanent and foundational that many individuals struggle to know how to answer the question. Actually, many individuals struggle to even understand the question.

In a world that so consistently values achievement, impact, and outcomes, I encounter many people who simply don't understand what it means to think about how they are being rather than what they are doing. I'll begin this chapter with an experience I had that has proven helpful in illuminating the concept in a vivid way.

As we'll see, a foundational tool in this work is inviting individuals to craft their own personal leadership mission statement. This effort to connect with and articulate one's deepest sense of purpose is an essential early step in any journey of personal growth. Significantly, the instructions for crafting this personal leadership mission statement include a requirement that individuals think about *how they want to be* – not just *what they want to do* – as leaders. I make it clear that goals, outcomes, and achievements are important, but this mission is meant to complement those things, not highlight them.

Several years ago, I was invited to offer a leadership development training at a prestigious business school. As usual, I invited the participants to craft their personal mission statements. I gave them a few minutes to work on a first draft, and when the writing time was up, I asked the class to discuss how they experienced the exercise. Immediately, one student's hand shot up with great enthusiasm. "I want to share my mission statement!" he exclaimed.

This was a bit unusual. We typically spend a few minutes talking about how it felt to craft these statements, whether it was easy or challenging, and whether it was unexplored terrain or something individuals have thought a lot about already. Most people hesitate to share their mission as giving voice to one's deepest sense of purpose is an act of vulnerability. Having someone request to share their mission with this immediacy and enthusiasm is not the norm.

I invited him to go ahead, and his statement was as clear and concise as could be: "My mission is to be a billionaire by the time I'm 40!", he said with utter confidence.

The class laughed a bit, responding – I suspect – to the blend of simplicity and audacity expressed in that incredibly brief and bold statement.

I let him know that I appreciated his clarity and enthusiasm but also told him that he had missed the essence of the exercise.

"That's a crystal-clear goal," I said. "But how are you going to be as you walk the path toward that outcome? Are you going to be known by everyone you encounter as a compassionate leader, amazing mentor, and deep listener who empowered others and left everyone you met feeling seen, heard, and appreciated? Or are you going to be known as a world-class jerk who manipulated and bullied everyone you met, leaving a trail of human wreckage along the path to your goal? It's important to have a goal, but your mission statement needs to speak to how you want to be as you walk the path toward your desired outcome."

The student had no immediate response to this comment, and it was clear he was going to have to do some more – and very different – reflection to honor the spirit of this exercise.

While this example of misunderstanding the essence of this exercise is particularly vivid, it's a fairly typical representation of how people often miss the point of this activity. When asked to reflect on how they want to be rather than what they want to do, many individuals struggle with the concept. In our world today, it remains rare to be invited to think in those terms, and many participants in these programs remark that this is not something they've really considered before, and they find it to be a hard concept to grasp.

A key benefit of the Flame model is that it makes it possible to talk about this dimension of our experience with new levels of clarity and rigor. Using the language of the Flame, it becomes possible to talk about the incident described above in the following way: That business school student was so focused on the "Do" and "Know" aspects of the work that he was in danger of neglecting the "Be" level of the Flame.

Again, there is nothing all that unusual about this situation. The "Do" aspect of any organization is publicly visible and undeniably mission critical. At City Year, millions of dollars of funding were contingent on demonstrating impact through getting things done. And there can be no doubt that what we Do is influenced by what we "Know" – our knowledge, skills, and competencies. In City Year's case, if an AmeriCorps member didn't know how to, say, multiply fractions and keep a student focused and on task, she was not going to be able to help her students improve their grades in math.

When we shift our attention to the BE aspect of the Flame, however, we find ourselves on terrain that is beyond what can be easily seen, measured, assessed, or taught. What exactly is the work to be done at the Be level? How do we develop people skillfully at that level of the Flame? Also, in a world where no external stakeholders are holding us accountable for doing this deep inner work, how do we cultivate the discipline to make it a priority amid all the other mission critical work to be done? And how do we do it without abandoning or ignoring the vital work at the DO and KNOW level of the Flame? In the absence of clear answers to those questions, many organizations don't even try to work at this level. Some may not even recognize this innermost level of our human experience exists.

It turns out that the leadership literature has something to say about our tendency to overlook, ignore, or underestimate the role that our innermost way of being plays in influencing the systems around us. In an influential essay entitled *The Blind Spot of Leadership*, MIT Professor Otto Scharmer explains it this way:

There is a blind spot in leadership theory, in the social sciences as well as in our everyday social experience. This blind spot concerns the inner place from which an action – what we do – originates... If we were to ask the question, "Where does our action come from?" most of us would be unable to provide an answer. The blind spot concerns the (inner) source from which we operate when we do what we do – the quality of attention that we use to relate to and bring forth the world.

I first began thinking about this blind spot when talking with the former CEO of Hanover Insurance, Bill O'Brien. He told me that his greatest insight after years of conducting organizational learning projects and facilitating corporate change was that "the success of an intervention depends on the interior condition of the intervener." That sentence struck a chord. What counts, it dawned on me, is not only what leaders do and how they do it, but that "interior condition," the inner place from which they operate. I also realized that organizations, institutions, and societies as a whole may have this blind spot – not only individuals. Maybe, it occurred to me, what really needs to be done in response to the current world crises – political, social, and spiritual – has to do with changing that interior condition: collectively shifting the inner place from which a person, an organization, or a system operates. (Scharmer, 2003)

It's a perspective that aligns powerfully with the Flame and Journey model presented here. If the events in the world around us are a reflection of our inner condition, then it follows that we must focus on shifting that innermost way of being as a prerequisite to shifting the systems and structures producing and sustaining the crises we see unfolding all around us today.

How, then, do we do this? How do we integrate a rigorous, intentional, and powerful focus on the inner dimensions of human experience along with our commitment to metrics, outcomes, and key performance indicators? *How do we develop individuals at the Be level of the Flame?*

Here's what I've learned: To do this work well, we need answers to two important questions:

1. What is the landscape of this inner terrain, and how do we illuminate it and guide others through it in ways that are both powerful and scalable?

2. What are the methods we must use to engage individuals in work at the "Be" level of the Flame?

After years of trial-and-error efforts to refine answers to these questions, I'm ready to share what I've learned.

ILLUMINATING THE INNER LANDSCAPE: JOSEPH CAMPBELL'S HERO'S JOURNEY

The journey of the hero is about the courage to seek the depths; the image of creative rebirth; the eternal cycle of change within us; the uncanny discovery that the seeker is the mystery which the seeker seeks to know. The hero's journey is a symbol that binds, in the original sense of the word, two distant ideas, the spiritual quest of the ancients with the modern search for identity. – The Hero's Journey: Joseph Campbell on His Life and Work (1990)

Who am I? Why am I here? How do I achieve my full potential?

The quest to find answers to these questions inevitably leads to an encounter with the scholar, sage, mentor, and guide who has illuminated the path to the answers to these questions for millions: Joseph Campbell.

Joseph Campbell was born in New York in 1904 and died in 1987. Over the course of his life, he became perhaps the most famous and influential comparative mythologist in the world. As a child he was fascinated by the stories and myths of Native Americans, and over time, his pursuit of that passion – as he would put it, his commitment to follow his bliss – opened up to an exploration of myths told by cultures around the world. He studied Norse mythology, Arthurian legends, tales of the Gods and Goddesses of ancient Egypt, Greece, the Aztec and Mayans; timeless myths from India, Japan, South America, Africa, the South Pacific, and much, much more.

Over time, Campbell came to discern themes that appeared again and again across wildly different cultural traditions. Ultimately, these insights coalesced into a discovery that underneath all the disparate stories humankind has been telling for millennia there lies a "monomyth" – a single story that we've been telling ourselves over and over and over again. In his seminal book originally published in 1949 entitled *The Hero With A Thousand Faces*, he laid out the pattern of what he chose to call the Hero's Journey (Campbell, 1949). It's a story that is ubiquitous and timeless, appearing again and again in the stories that we continue to tell in modern Hollywood blockbusters.

I first encountered Campbell's work in 2004, at the age of 33 when I participated in an intense personal growth experience called the New Warrior Training Adventure (NWTA), run by an organization called The ManKind Project. I was in the fifth year of my doctoral program, and I was not in a good place. I spent many of my young adult years struggling with a lack of direction and an uncertainty about how to channel my idealism and passion to do good in the world. In my 20s, I was what I have come to call a *Lost Idealist:* I burned with a passion to create positive change and felt a desperate need to live a life of purpose, meaning, and impact but had no idea how to do that. And the fear that I would never find my path and would squander my potential gnawed at my soul every day.

I recognize now that I was terrified of taking some conventional path that would lead to material comfort and social acceptability but would fail to fulfill my soul's yearning to live a life of purpose and positive impact. In a real sense, the choice to go to grad school to get a masters and then a doctorate provided a way to continue my search for meaning while delaying the need to make a concrete and seemingly irrevocable career choice. Although I had decided to pursue a doctorate, I didn't have an interest in working in academia, and as I approached the end of my doctoral work, the fact that I still didn't have clarity about what path to walk filled me with genuine despair. It is one thing to feel lost as a 22-year-old undergrad; the possibility that I would find myself 12 years later as a 34-year-old with a doctorate and – still! – no clear sense of direction was, quite literally, horrifying. Was I doomed to spend my entire life tortured by indecision, feeling that I was squandering my potential as I stumbled through a dark forest with no idea where I was, why I was here, or where I should go?

That was the increasingly desperate state of my soul when two beloved cousins of mine encouraged me to check out an experience called the NWTA. They had both completed the program and found it to be life-changing, and they strongly encouraged me to sign up. Operating on the belief that "if you do what you've always done, you'll get what you've already got," I decided to take the risk and give it a go.

The NWTA is designed to be a "rite of passage" experience that is grounded in the three key stages of the Hero's Journey: *Separation, Initiation, and Return.* Here's how that works:

It occurred at a rural retreat center where we were physically separated from anyone not involved in the program, and we were required to turn off our phones and not make contact with the outside world for the duration of the program.

Separation

During our time at the center, we were faced with a series of tests and trials: While some of them involved physical challenges, the most difficult involved opportunities to confront our own inner "shadow" – the doubts, fears, wounds, and struggles that held us back, kept us frightened and small, and prevented us from living up to our full potential. Without going into the details of what this involved, I will simply say that this involved turning inwards to directly confront personal wounds and fears buried so deep in my soul that I had gone years hardly recognizing their existence. Surfacing and working with those fears was some of the most deep and profound work I have ever participated in or witnessed. I found it to be life-changing; as this book makes clear, insights and ideas learned that weekend have become central to my work and my ability to live the life of purpose and meaning that my soul always craved. I know that many other participants felt the same way.

Initiation

Once we made it through those experiences of initiation, we engaged in rituals designed to honor our emergence from those trials and our transformation into higher, more fully realized versions of ourselves. We were then given a chance to reflect on the gifts we had received from our journey and were challenged to craft our own Personal Leadership Mission – and our own related Shadow Mission – to guide our efforts to put those gifts to work serving others in the months and years ahead.

Return

While there was a lot about that experience that was transformational, without a doubt the element that had the deepest impact on my life and work was the encounter with the work of Joseph Campbell. Discovering the Hero's Journey was like finding the map to the journey I'd been on for decades. I have already mentioned how, in resisting the choice to embark on a conventional career path that might have provided both material comfort and social acceptance, I had felt for years like I was lost in a forest with no clear idea of where to go or like I was stuck in a labyrinth I could not escape. After years of feeling isolated and alone in that experience, imagine how I felt when I read these words from Joseph Campbell about how it feels to embark on the Hero's Journey:

> *You enter the forest at the darkest point, where there is no path. Where there is a way or a path, it is*

*someone else's path; each human being is a unique
phenomenon. The idea is to find your own pathway
to bliss. (2004, p. xvii)*

The sense of having my innermost experience be seen,
understood, and validated was profound. It transformed me
from a lost, fearful, and isolated grad student into a courageous soul who for years – without understanding exactly
what he was doing – had been striving to bravely walk a path
of spiritual growth and awakening. I also had the sense of
discovering, to my amazement, that the path I was on led not
to isolation and profound loneliness but to a sense of
connection with all of humanity, with everyone across all
boundaries of time and culture who had chosen to walk a
similar path. Campbell puts it this way:

*We have not even to risk the adventure alone for the
heroes of all time have gone before us. The labyrinth
is thoroughly known...we have only to follow the
thread of the hero path. And where we had thought
to find an abomination we shall find a God. And
where we had thought to slay another we shall slay
ourselves. Where we had thought to travel outwards
we shall come to the center of our own existence.
And where we had thought to be alone we shall be
with all the world. (1949, p. 25)*

Heady stuff. *Mystical* stuff. Even as I write this, I experience concern that for many readers, the notion of discovering
a God within the self and experiencing communion with the
world may be too far out, too esoteric, and too hippy trippy to
tolerate. Yet it would be dishonest to back away from this
language to suggest that it didn't evoke a profound sense in
me of being seen and known at the deepest levels. Of course,
Campbell himself explained that experience best. He states:

> *The function of (heroic) symbols is to give you a*
> *sense of Aha! Yes, I know what it is, it's myself.*
> *(Collins, 1997)*

This encounter with Campbell through the NWTA launched me on several years of what can properly be called an obsession with his work. In the years following that weekend, I read almost every word he has ever written, devoured a biography about his life, and became a passionate student of how his work has influenced both popular culture and the work of others in the human potential movement (the effort to cram Campbell's work down the throat of City Year AmeriCorps members described in Chapter 1 occurred during this phase of my life). Once I began looking, I found Campbell's work everywhere: from Oprah to Brene Brown, from Deepak Chopra to Otto Scharmer, from George Lucas to JK Rowling, and on and on and on. The stories we tell ourselves today in the early years of the 21st century are just the latest riffs on the story humankind has been telling itself over and over again for all of recorded history. Essentially everyone I have read or encountered working in the realm of human transformation references Campbell's work.

Here, then, is the landscape of the interior, the path each of us must walk to develop ourselves at the BE level of the Flame. Campbell illuminates the blind spot, revealing the journey each of us must take to become our truest selves. As a scholar, my leadership development studies had led me to a recognition of the deeply interconnected nature of inner change and outer change. As a human being, I had had my own experience of the power of turning inwards to confront myself, and how that journey of self-discovery had illuminated the pathway out of self-limiting patterns and cycles I had been trapped in for years. And today, as a leadership development practitioner, I have arrived at the conviction that any effort to create change that does not operate at this level is, quite simply, limited in highly problematic ways. To not work at this level is to ignore or misunderstand the journey each individual must undertake to live up to their fullest potential represents a failure to appreciate the interconnectedness of change within the self and change in the world around us.

The NWTA experience left me with some burning questions. The program engaged about 30 participants and the roughly same number of staff in a three and a half day gathering at a secluded retreat center. Was there a way to create some kind of similar transformational experience on a larger scale? Was there a way to invite individuals into the Hero's Journey without requiring them to head off into the woods for days at a time?

While I am a huge fan of personal growth retreats, I was keenly aware of the problems of seeking to recreate these kinds of experiences as a strategy for promoting large-scale change. Among the subset of individuals who were at all interested in these experiences, surely only a handful had the time and resources to step away from their lives for days at a time to participate in these kinds of programs. Also, a whole lot of people – perhaps the majority – had no interest in this sort of experience at all. Finally, the world was full of people working at the front lines of change in all kinds of fields: teachers, medical professionals, social workers, nonprofit staff, police officers, soldiers, social entrepreneurs, and so much more. On the one hand, I was convinced that individuals in all of these roles could only access their full potential to bring about positive change by engaging in this "Be" level work in some manner. On the other hand, the idea that all of these folks would head off to complete intense multi-day personal growth experiences was just not realistic.

There had to be some way to engage large numbers of individuals in this kind of work and to build it into the daily life of organizations and institutions. It would have to be properly calibrated, of course; in the quest for scale, there would surely have to be a trade-off in depth and intensity. But if this kind of deep inner work was essential to creating real change, then it was vital to find a way to build a capacity to do this work into organizations at scale.

In Chapters 1 and 2, I shared the story of my trial-and-error efforts to develop an approach to inner work that was effective at a large-scale organization. The struggles to overcome resistance, find ways to invite skeptical participants into these spaces, and present Campbell's Hero's Journey framework in ways that were productive and not off-putting are all chronicled there. Here, I'll expand upon the perspective shared in Chapter 2 by saying more about the content of the programming designed to develop individuals at the "Be" level of the Flame.

It's important to note that the essential element of the Hero's Journey is the confrontation with one's deepest, truest self. This was the essence of the encounter with the "shadow" at the heart of the NWTA programming, and it is fundamentally about embracing our own wholeness. The insight here is that the journey to self-knowledge, self-mastery, and self-love all require the emotionally and spiritually demanding work of seeing our full selves, including the shadow parts of ourselves that cause us embarrassment and shame. On the inner journey, we must come face to face with ourselves and discover essential truths and untapped potential hidden within us.

The implication of this truth is that most of us, most of the time, wander through the ordinary, everyday world as strangers to ourselves. We may be competent and successful to varying degrees, but our understanding of ourselves is incomplete. We simply don't truly know who we are unless we

decide to take the journey, turn inwards, and do the work
required to confront and claim our inner wholeness.

CONFRONTING THE SHADOW

How can I be substantial if I do not cast a shadow?
I must have a dark side also if I am to be whole.
– Carl Jung (1933, p. 35)

While crafting a Personal Leadership Mission statement is
important work, it is vital to understand that it is, ultimately,
only a partial and incomplete effort to confront the self. To truly
develop at the "Be" level of the Flame, we must go further in our
journey of encountering the self. In this exercise, we are invited to
craft – and own – our Personal *Shadow Mission*.

This exercise is grounded in the recognition that every light –
every Flame – casts a shadow: A dark region where our light does
not reach. In terms of leadership development, this means that we
all have the potential to act in ways that are not in alignment with
our mission. The more clear and courageous we are in confronting what it means to be out of alignment with our mission,
the more conscious we can be about not sliding onto that path.

As mentioned previously, this understanding of the shadow
is deeply grounded in the work of Swiss psychologist Carl
Jung (Joseph Campbell was a student of Jung's and edited a
posthumous collection of Jung's works, so there is a deep
connection between their work). Jung felt that becoming
conscious of the shadow was an essential step for anyone
seeking genuine self-knowledge; quite simply, anyone who
hadn't done this work didn't actually understand themselves
and lived in a sort of permanent state of partial consciousness
and disconnection from self. The reasons why we might resist

this effort are easy to grasp: This is hard work and is, by definition, uncomfortable, scary, and unsettling. There is a very real possibility we might emerge from this process with our understanding of ourselves altered...perhaps even shattered. This is why the confrontation with the self – with the whole self – is such a spiritual trial. Jung explains it this way:

> *The shadow is a moral problem that challenges the whole ego-personality, for no one can become conscious of the shadow without considerable moral effort. To become conscious of it involves recognizing the dark aspect of the personality as present and real. This act is the essential condition for any kind of self-knowledge, and it therefore, as a rule, meets with considerable resistance. (1976, p. 145)*

He also states:

> *This confrontation is the first test of courage on the inner way, a test sufficient to frighten off most people, for the meeting with ourselves belongs to the more unpleasant things that can be avoided so long as we can project everything negative into the environment. (1976, p. 147)*

This concept of "projection" is critical. Jung is saying that if we haven't integrated the parts of ourselves that we don't like into our own understanding of ourselves, then we project that darkness and negativity onto some "other," and we believe – with an intense certainty – that they possess all the negative traits that we refuse to recognize within ourselves. It's a psychological trick the mind plays – not consciously, of course – that allows us to rest comfortably in the illusion that "we" are purely good and virtuous, and "they" are fundamentally evil, sinful, and dangerous.

There can be no doubt that this phenomenon has played a pivotal role in the darkest chapters in human history. Consider the evils of Nazi Germany: In the mind of a Nazi, "we" were noble Aryans, ideal in body, mind, and spirit. "They" – the Jews – were evil incarnate: subhuman vermin paradoxically exercising nefarious control over government, media, and finance, hellbent on destroying all that is good and holy in the world. Consider, also, the way African Americans have long been viewed over the course of American history. In the white supremacist worldview that has endured from the earliest days of slavery through Jim Crow segregation through our current era of mass incarceration, white Christian Americans are pure, patriotic, and fundamentally decent. African Americans and other people of color are subhuman beasts who are lazy, untrustworthy, and driven by uncontrollable urges to act as violent sexual predators.

It's important to see clearly what is going on here. The institution of slavery involved brutal, horrific violence by white people against Black people, including whippings, lynching, and torture. Yet the phenomenon of projection allowed white Americans to rest in the illusion that it was Black people, not white people, who were violent. We know that sexual violence against slaves was common; white males could and did rape slaves at will. Projection allowed white Americans to believe themselves to be chaste and in control of their sexual urges while believing Black people to be sexual predators. And we know that slaves were forced to work relentlessly, often engaged in the harshest manual labor with subsistence meals, while slave owners lived lives of vastly greater leisure and comfort. Projection allowed white Americans to see themselves as hard working and deserving of hard-earned comforts while believing Black people to be lazy seekers of benefits they had not earned and were not entitled to enjoy.

We must have no illusions: this projection of unexplored shadow is alive and well and is one of the most powerful forces in our politics today. We must remember that Donald Trump launched his successful first Presidential campaign by declaring that Mexicans seeking to enter America were "drug dealers, criminals, and rapists" and won a second term by doubling down on claims that illegal immigrants were eating cats and dogs in the suburbs of the heartland. He regularly accused his political opponents of illegal activities that he himself has committed, like weaponizing the judicial system against political rivals. A narrow majority of Americans believed him. The shadow – both personal and collective – is alive and well in America and around the world right now.

Jung notes that this demonization of the other is accompanied by a disconnection from reality and objective truth. It is as though the unwillingness to see the truth within our inner worlds produces an unwillingness to see the truth in the world around us. Jung explains it this way:

> It is often tragic to see how blatantly a man bungles his own life and the lives of others yet remains totally incapable of seeing how much the whole tragedy originates in himself, and how he continuously feeds it and keeps it going. Not consciously, of course–for consciously he is engaged in bewailing and cursing a faithless world that recedes further and further into the distance. Rather, it is an unconscious factor which spins the illusions that veils his world. And what is being spun is a cocoon, which in the end will completely envelop him. (1976, p. 147)

Jung is discussing an individual experience, but as we have seen throughout history, when this inner condition exists in large numbers of people it produces a collective detachment from reality with national and global implications. Large numbers of individuals cocoon themselves in an illusion impervious to facts and scornful of objective reality. Personally, I find it impossible to read this text and not see its relevance to the dramatic growth of conspiracy theories like Q-Anon that we have seen gain influence in recent years in this country. The belief that the world is controlled by a Satan-worshiping cabal of cannibalistic pedophiles surely counts as an "illusion that veils [the]world."

This kind of detachment from reality represents a genuine threat to civic life here in America and around the world. Any effort to address the many challenges of our moment needs to include an understanding of why so many people embrace lies and conspiracy theories and what might be done to respond to the trend.

With Jung's illumination of the shadow and his explanation of why so many individuals resist walking the path toward achieving this inner wholeness, we have a theory of the problem, along with a path forward. If avoiding the shadow and living in a state of disconnection from self leads to the embrace of these kinds of all-encompassing illusions, then guiding people on the path back toward connection and wholeness is an effort that we must dedicate ourselves to in the years ahead. Every time an individual achieves a higher consciousness of their wholeness, they gain the ability to work skillfully and consciously with some of what they have been projecting out into the world onto the "other." In this way, each of us has the opportunity – and I would argue the responsibility – to reduce in some small but meaningful way the power of that dark energy in our collective lives.

This understanding of human nature challenges a deep assumption of Western civilization. There is a foundational belief here in the West that we are all rational, independent individuals whose choices are guided by reason and logic. The assumption of this worldview is this: *If people encounter data or facts that challenge their views, then they will change their views to fit the facts.* As our daily headlines make abundantly clear, this is not the way people work. Recent research actually reveals that individuals who encounter facts that challenge their current beliefs actually get *more* committed – not less – to those existing beliefs (Beck, 2019). The assumption that we are rational actors whose behavior is driven by reason and logic is deeply flawed.

If we embrace the work of Campbell and Jung, however, we arrive at a different understanding of humankind. We are beings with the capacity to develop and evolve, and as such we have the potential to transcend our current level of consciousness and arrive at greater depths of self-awareness and higher levels of personal responsibility. We all arrive at adulthood to some degree disconnected from our true selves, yet there is a path we can walk to achieve a state of genuine wholeness. But we can only achieve that potential and access that wholeness if we personally choose to undertake the difficult task of confronting the shadow within ourselves. This requires confronting the jarring truth that all kinds of darkness we have long assumed existed "out there" can be found "in here" – inside the self. Along the way, we are sure to discover the universal human truth that we all contain both light and dark within the self. And in seeing and accepting the truth of our own wholeness, we attain the ability to see that same wholeness in others. In this way, we withdraw our projections and awaken from the illusion created and sustained by our earlier, more limited level of consciousness.

We should not be surprised that vast numbers of individuals have not yet done this work. This is hard work and – as Jung makes clear – every individual has good reasons to resist walking this path. It's important to emphasize, though, that this Flame and Journey approach is based on an equally important truth: Surely, another reason why so few people have taken this journey is because so few individuals have been invited to embark upon it and be guided skillfully on the path.

In my work, I am continually amazed at how many people have never been invited to think about their own shadow. Over the years, I have led trainings for thousands of people including idealistic young people; graduates of Ivy league schools; highly experienced executives; elite military personnel; and deeply committed and engaged civic leaders running for every office from school board to Congress. I've delivered trainings on this concept in the United States, India, Bangladesh, Israel, and Europe. For the vast majority of participants – I would estimate around 85–90% – these trainings are the first time they have ever been invited to explore their own shadow.

This is no longer acceptable. I believe that we have hit the limits of our abilities to respond meaningfully to the challenges of this moment without confronting the shadow in intentional and skillful ways. This unexplored and unexamined dark energy is impacting our civic life here in America and abroad in powerful ways and will only grow stronger until we turn to face it and work with it in productive ways at both the individual and collective levels.

This is challenging work that requires courage and creativity. The good news, though, is that it is possible. Over the course of years of experimentation, I have refined an approach to inviting people to work with shadow in ways that are scalable and carefully calibrated to be effective in professional environments. It is not necessary for everyone to head off to a retreat center for an expensive and immersive personal growth seminar. We can engage productively in this work in conference rooms and meeting spaces during the work day, in ways that are impactful, safe, and productive. We can build an organizational capacity to guide large numbers of people through a journey that includes confronting shadow, ensuring that we can work productively with this dark energy as individuals, organizations, and as a society.

Perhaps if we invited more people into this work and guided them skillfully along the path to wholeness, we might begin to see a meaningful reduction in the power of the shadow to warp and toxify our civic life. Perhaps we might find our way beyond the polarization, partisanship, detachment from reality that is threatening our democracy. Perhaps we might grow beyond the limited, problematic ways of being that are calling forth and creating so much of the conflict and chaos we see all around us today.

As Carl Jung says, "One does not become enlightened by imagining figures of light, but by making the darkness conscious." (1968, p. 99)

MAKING IT PRACTICAL

So what does it look like to guide individuals through this inner journey in practical and scalable ways? How do we engage individuals in this work in ways that are calibrated to be acceptable in the organizational conference room rather than the therapist's office or the personal growth retreat? Over the course of several years of experimentation, I arrived at a set of three exercises that invite individuals to do this work in a way that is deep and meaningful but also appropriate for the workplace. In time, I came to see these exercises as the core of this effort to develop people at the "Be" level of the Flame. The exercises are as follows:

- Core Values

- Personal Leadership Mission Statement

- Shadow Mission

Here's how it all works:

Core Values Exercise

Our core values represent our own deepest beliefs and highest aspirations. They should serve as our North Star, empowering us to live and lead with both clarity and integrity while confronting complexity and uncertainty. Getting clear on our own personal core values is an essential first step on any journey of personal growth.

For this activity, individuals are invited to generate a list of values (usually 3–8, but there are no hard rules here) that are absolutely essential to them and that speak to their deepest beliefs and highest aspirations.

The guidelines we provide for this exercise are as follows:

- Distill the Essence
  The work of developing a list of core values often involves sifting through layers of vaguely articulated sentiments and beliefs. It should feel a bit like inner archeology; you are digging down through layers until you uncover that which is most essential and foundational. When you look at your final list, you should see nothing that feels like a marginal commitment or shallow belief; what remains is a list of the values that are absolutely essential and central to you.

- Be Comprehensive
  While striving to include only the most essential values, be mindful that this list should also be comprehensive in the sense that it reflects you in the fullest and most complete sense. Nothing essential should be omitted, and the final list should reflect all of the core values that inform your leadership.

- Be Clear

  Each individual word or phrase on your final list should represent a unique, clearly articulated value. Be sure to push past work that is almost – but not completely – clear. For example, it is not unusual for a first draft of core values to include some phrases like "Equality/Justice" or "Empathy/Kindness." While concepts like "Equality" and "Justice" are related, they are not identical. And the concepts of "Empathy" and "Kindness" are actually quite distinct. Push yourself to decide which of these terms speaks most powerfully to the core value you are trying to express; if both feel essential, list them as two separate values on your list. The goal is a list of core values in which each item on the list is unique, distinct, and clearly stated.

- Complement Each Word or Phrase With a Brief Explanatory Statement

  A fully developed list of core values includes a set of words or phrases that state the values, complemented by brief explanatory phrases that provide deeper insight into exactly what those words or phrases mean to you. This is necessary because it is not enough to be clear about your values; you need to be able to communicate what those values mean to you in a clear and compelling way.

In an effort to both share an example of what this looks and provide some insight into the values that guide me in my leadership development work, here's my list:

- *Family* – Nurturing and supporting my family to feel unconditionally loved and to develop into our best selves is my highest value.

- *Service* – Using my gifts and abilities to improve the lives of others gives me purpose and meaning and is the highest use of my potential.

- *Integrity* – I strive to live in alignment with my deepest beliefs and core values, even when doing so is challenging.

- *Courage* – I strive to bravely take purposeful action in the face of fear and uncertainty.

- *Compassion* – I seek to offer a deep sense of love, acceptance, and kindness to myself and others I meet on the path.

- *Curiosity* – I strive to live with an openness to new ideas and new insights and to never stop learning, exploring, and asking questions.

- *Creativity* – I will dedicate time to bringing art, music, truth and beauty into the world for as long as I live.

Personal Leadership Mission Statement Exercise

Once you have established your core values, the next task is to craft your own Personal Leadership Mission Statement. This brief, clear mission statement will articulate your highest aspirations regarding who you want to be as a leader.

With this exercise, you are called to clearly express thoughts and feelings that too often remain vague and unformed. There is great power in this clarity. Once you clearly articulate your highest aspirations for yourself as a leader, you are able to hold yourself accountable on a daily basis and push yourself to develop toward your own vision of who you aspire to be. Equally important, because everyone who meets you can sense the presence – or absence – of this inner clarity, this work has a profound impact on your ability to connect with, inspire, and engage others.

This short, clear statement should capture the essence of how you want to be in the world. Guidelines for writing a leadership mission statement are as follows:

- It should begin with the phrase, "My leadership mission is...."

- Distill the essence, don't write an essay.

- It should include the qualities of character that you hope to embody as you walk your path.

- Your mission should speak to both *how you want to be* AND *what you want to do* in the world. In other words, it should speak not only to outcomes you want to create in the world but also to how you aspire to be as you walk the path toward creating those outcomes.

- Finally, this mission statement should be larger than any job or role you currently hold or aspire to hold in the future. For this exercise, you are invited to connect to your deepest sense of mission as a human being. You will hopefully express that mission through roles you hold in your life, but the mission should not be attached to any particular role you may fill.

Here is mine:

> *My leadership mission is to practice courage and compassion in honoring – and helping others to honor – the sacred interdependence of our world.*

I encourage individuals to try setting a timer and write this in four minutes. Those who need more time are of course welcome to take it, but I have seen again and again that some very powerful work can be completed with just a few minutes of intense focus.

Shadow Mission Exercise

Our Personal Leadership Mission invites us to connect with our light. Once we've done that, we are ready to engage in the related work of confronting our own personal shadow.

We do this by inviting individuals to complete an exercise that we call the Personal Shadow Mission. The instructions are as follows:

- It should begin with the phrase "My shadow mission is…."

- It should articulate the choices you make when you choose not to align your actions with your leadership mission.

- Note that a shadow often results from the *withholding of light*, as opposed to the *spreading of darkness*. In other words, if part of your mission is an intention to "spread love," the choice to not align with that mission is a choice to "withhold love," and not to "spread hate."

- A clear Shadow Mission should "get you in the gut." You should encounter it as an accurate description of a way of being that you recognize within yourself but is uncomfortable and unpleasant to confront.

Here's how this works for me. Once again, my mission is as follows:

> *My leadership mission is to practice courage and compassion in honoring – and helping others to honor – the sacred interdependence of our world.*

Now here's the related shadow mission:

> *My shadow mission is to practice cowardice and disconnection in disregarding – and helping others to disregard – the sacred interdependence of our world.*

In Chapter 2, I told the story of my decision to bring the shadow concept to City Year. When we own our shadow on the individual level, we strengthen our ability to lead from the light and consciously minimize the influence the shadow has on our life and leadership. When we do this work together with others, we become a community engaged in a collective effort to work skillfully and effectively with the shadow. We are no longer isolated and alone in this work; we recognize that all of us – every human being – has a shadow that is a foundational part of the self. Inevitably, these conversations surface a wealth of wisdom regarding how to live our mission and not our shadow, how to work skillfully with our shadow, and how to make peace with our own wholeness. Watching groups of individuals discuss and explore these matters with wisdom and compassion has become my favorite part of doing this work.

THE METHOD: CREATING AND HOLDING SPACES THAT CREATE CONDITIONS FOR INNER TRANSFORMATION

No [person] is great enough or wise enough for any of us to surrender our destiny to. The only way in which anyone can lead us is to restore to us the belief in our own guidance. – Henry Miller

Once we understand the nature of the work to be done at the innermost "Be" level of the Flame on both conceptual and practical terms, we confront the question of how to make it happen effectively at scale. How do we invite large numbers of people into the inward journey? How do we support individuals to step into the role of Guide effectively? How do we even think about engaging in this work?

The first step, I have learned, is to illuminate at a deep level the paradigm of leadership that individuals must embrace to be effective in this work. Because the word "leadership" can mean utterly different things to different people, it is important to make it clear that when it comes to the "Be" level of the Flame, our work is to "lead" in the sense highlighted in the Henry Miller quote above. Our challenge is to lead others to a restored or renewed belief in their own inner strength, wisdom, and insight.

This may be a very different understanding of leadership than what we currently hold. If we believe that leadership involves influencing others to accept our own understanding of reality or do what we tell them to do, then we will make very poor guides. If we understand leadership to be providing others with answers or solving their problems, then our actions will be the exact opposite of what they should be in this work. If we understand leadership to be the settling of disagreements and the maintenance of order and tranquility, then we are likely to fail in guiding others through inner work.

Ironically, all of these ways of thinking about leadership are grounded in the ancient myth of the hero – a lone individual with a superhuman ability to understand and control events in a chaotic world. The hero walks through the world as a solitary, isolated individual who rides into town, Lone Ranger style, and single handedly "fixes" major problems before riding off into the sunset to "save" another community of helpless strangers. Everything about this heroic myth is problematic when it comes to engaging individuals in the inner work at the "Be" level of the Flame.

In an essay called *Leadership in the Age of Complexity: From Hero to Host*, leadership experts Margaret Wheatley and Debbie Frieze explain the paradigm shift that we must make here in the way we conceptualize leadership. They state:

> *Heroic leadership rests on the illusion that someone can be in control. Yet we live in a world of complex systems whose very existence means that they are inherently uncontrollable. No one is in charge of our food systems. No one is in charge of our schools. No one is in charge of the environment...No one is in charge! These systems are emergent phenomena – the result of thousands of small, local actions that converge to create powerful systems with properties that may bear little or no resemblance to the smaller actions that gave rise to them...If we want to be able to get these complex systems to work better, we need to abandon our reliance on the leader-as-hero and invite in the leader-as-host...These leaders-as-hosts are candid enough to admit that they don't know what to do; they realize that it is sheer foolishness to rely on them for answers. But they also know that they can trust in other people's creativity and commitment to get the work done. They know that other people, no matter where they are in the organizational hierarchy, can be as motivated, diligent, and creative as the leader, given the right invitation. (2010, p. 2)*

In our trainings for facilitators who will be guiding others through inner work, we present the two paradigms as seen in Table 1.

Those who seek to facilitate inner work are called to be leaders in this sense of Leader as Host. Their job is to offer a steady stream of invitations to the members of their groups: They must invite others to connect with their own deepest sources of motivation and to explore in an ongoing way

Table 1. Overview of "Leader as Hero" and "Leader as Host" Frameworks.

Leader as Hero	Leader as Host
• Provides the answers	• Asks key questions
• Solve problems for others	• Invites others to explore challenges
• Provides direction and control	• Creates a space for others to fill
• Has nothing more to learn	• Is also learning every day

whether they are living with integrity to their values and mission. It is essential to recognize that others cannot be compelled to do this work, and it can't be done for them; none of us can truly know if someone else is living with integrity or not. The work is to offer the invitation and create and hold a space that allows others to engage in this work, should they choose to accept the invitation.

Given the importance of the concept of "creating and holding space" to this work, we have found it helpful to highlight four different tools we can use in our efforts to create and hold space. We call them the "Four Pathways." Here is an overview:

1. *Physical Space:* The first pathway involves hosting discussions in spaces that are free from distractions and that are conducive to reflection and thoughtful dialogue. Conversations held in spaces that are quiet, comfortable, and private are sure to unfold in different ways than conversations held

in public spaces like coffee shops or outside in a busy park. In the era of COVID-19 when all of this programming has moved online, the meaning of physical space shifts but is still relevant. Is the video image and sound clear? Is the background free of distractions? Thoughtful consideration of these matters is one key pathway to creating space.

2. *Temporal Space:* The second pathway involves using time as a powerful boundary. When we make it a point to start and end our groups on time and stick to a clear agenda, we send a clear message that time is both important and limited. When time is used in a deliberate and intentional way, participants understand that they must either use this time productively while they are in it…or a sacred opportunity for learning, growth, and connection has been lost.

3. *Psychological Space:* The third pathway requires launching each group with a clear message that everyone in the group is responsible for the quality of learning that will happen in this space. The primary tool for creating this kind of psychological space is an exercise that we call the Group Learning Agreement, which invites everyone to articulate their own goals for the group, the values they commit to upholding in these discussions, and any logistical agreements that participants want to codify. Once this agreement is crafted, everyone understands that each individual in the group has a role to play in upholding that agreement. Should any violations of the agreement occur, the group needs to work together to decide how to proceed. A second key tool we have found to be invaluable in creating psychological space is the concept of "Challenge by Choice." This simple yet powerful term makes it clear that nobody will ever be compelled to disclose personal matters against their own will or judgment. It's a way of inviting

participation while affirming that individuals are in charge of their own boundaries at every moment in the process.

4. *Spiritual Space:* The fourth and final pathway involves highlighting the insight that the inner way of being of facilitators influences these spaces in powerful yet mysterious ways. When they are fully present, awake, and deeply engaged in the dynamics of the group, the group will sense that quality of presence. When they are distracted, disengaged, or dismissive of the work occurring in the space, participants will sense that quality of presence as well. Individuals involved in creating these spaces must recognize the deep truth that has been explored at length in this approach to leadership: The world we create around us represents a reflection of our inner state as leaders, so we must strive to follow the guidance of Gandhi and "be the change we wish to see in the world." This is spiritual work that is as important and impactful as it is mysterious and unquantifiable.

THE GOALS OF WORK AT THE BE LEVEL OF THE FLAME: INSIGHT, INTEGRITY, AND VERTICAL DEVELOPMENT

As is hopefully clear at this point, spaces focused on work at the Be level of the Flame are not about problem solving, action planning, program execution or discussing deliverables. Neither are these spaces focused on knowledge transfer or skill-building. All of that work is important and ideally happens with excellence at other times and in other spaces in every organization. This space, though, needs to focus on work that is related but distinct. The desired outcomes of these

"BE" level spaces fall into three categories: *Insight, Integrity and Vertical Development.* Here's what those terms mean:

- *Insight:* According to the dictionary, insight is "the act of or outcome of grasping the inward or hidden nature of things." As previously discussed, we cannot give people inner clarity around matters like their core values, leadership mission, and shadow mission. Our goal should be to create conditions in which individuals are able to achieve *insight* into their own personal truths related to those exercises. The challenge is to create spaces in which the noise of the world fades away, distractions disappear, and individuals have a chance to listen for the quiet voice of truth whispering in their souls. Of course, insight is of little use if it does not directly animate our daily action, which brings us to our second goal.

- *Integrity:* According to the dictionary, integrity is defined in the following ways: "1. the quality of being honest and having strong moral principles; moral uprightness. 2. the state of being whole and undivided." Once individuals have done the work to get clear on matters like their core values, mission and shadow, then the ever-present question becomes: Am I living with integrity to my own inner truths as I walk my path? Work at the "BE" level of the Flame requires continually inviting individuals to reflect on this simple yet profound question. Again, we can't provide anyone with the answers to these important questions, but we can create and hold spaces that invite them to discover the answers within themselves.

- *Vertical Development:* This was a concept that we encountered in the chapter on "DO and KNOW" and it speaks to an effort to support individuals to "earn a bigger mind." It represents an alternative to "horizontal development," which involves simply gaining new skills and knowledge. The idea is that within the containers we create for work to occur at the "BE" level of the Flame, we are holding spaces in which individuals ask new questions, grapple with new perspectives, and engage with complexity in sustained and productive ways. We're very clear that the goal in these spaces is not to arrive at simple answers, solve problems, or wrap up complex issues in neat little bows. Rather than the focus on outcomes and actions in the outer world, the goal is creating the kinds of experiences of engaging with complexity that we know we must undertake if we seek to "earn a bigger mind."

FINAL THOUGHTS ON THE BE LEVEL OF THE FLAME

There is, to be sure, much more that could be said here. When we dive deep into the inner world, we find ourselves in terrain that has been explored for millennia by religion, myth, and philosophy and for centuries by modern disciplines like psychology, anthropology, organizational development, and leadership. Equally important, this chapter merely scratches the surface of the practice of creating spaces that invite inner work in skillful and effective ways. While there is much more that could be said, my hope is that I have provided enough depth and detail here to illuminate this inner world and the tools that make it possible to engage in large-scale inner development in useful ways. I'll bring this chapter to a close with the following final thoughts.

In his book *Modern Man in Search of a Soul*, Jung includes a chapter entitled "The Spiritual Problem of Modern Man." He explains our predicament as follows (here I'll add a caveat that I've preserved the gendered language of his original writing in order to not overly complicate the language, but I invite readers to understand this to be talking about all of humankind):

> *I must say that the man we call modern, the man who is aware of the immediate present, is by no means the average man. He is rather the man who stands up on a peak, or at the very edge of the world, the abyss of the future before him, above him the heavens, and below him the whole of mankind with a history that disappears in primeval mists. The modern man – or, let us say again, the man of the immediate present – is rarely met with. There are few who live up to the name, for they must be conscious to a superlative degree. Since to be wholly of the present means to be fully conscious of one's existence as a man, it requires the most intensive and extensive consciousness, with a minimum of unconsciousness. It must be clearly understood that the mere fact of living in the present does not make a man modern, for in that case everyone at present alive would be so. He alone is modern who is fully conscious of the present. (1933, pp. 196–197)*

At this moment when we face a multitude of existential crises – all self-created – unfolding simultaneously, surely the time is ripe to hear this message. If our environment is in crisis, surely it is because for too long we have lived in a state of unconsciousness regarding the impact of our present choices on the natural world around us. If we find ourselves yet again struggling to achieve racial justice and equality after 250 years as a nation, surely it is because for too long too many of us have lived in a state of unconsciousness regarding the racist ideology that has been part of our nation since its founding. If we find ourselves living together on a fragile planet having developed the technology to destroy civilization many times over while continuing to act under the illusion that there actually is an "us" and a "them," surely it is because for too long we have lived in a state of unconsciousness regarding the need to integrate light and shadow within ourselves.

In his book *The Social Animal*, journalist David Brooks suggests that this lack of consciousness regarding our true inner state is a key reason why so many of our efforts to address complex public problems have failed. He states:

> *[O]ver the past generations we have seen big policies yield disappointing results. Since 1983, we've reformed the education system again and again, yet more than a quarter of high-school students drop out, even though all rational incentives tell them not to. We've tried to close the gap between white and Black achievement but have failed. We've spent a generation enrolling more young people in college without understanding why so many don't graduate.*
>
> *One could go on: We've tried feebly to reduce widening inequality. We've tried to boost economic mobility. We've tried to stem the tide of children raised in single-parent homes. We've tried to reduce the polarization that marks our politics. We've tried to ameliorate the boom-and-bust cycle of our economies. In recent decades, the world has tried to export capitalism to Russia, plant democracy in the Middle East, and boost development in Africa. And the results of these efforts are mostly disappointing.*
>
> *These failures have been marked by a single feature: Reliance on an overly simplistic view of human nature. ... Many of the policies were proposed by wonks who are comfortable only with traits and*

> *correlations that can be measured and*
> *quantified....They were executed by officials that*
> *have only the most superficial grasp of what is*
> *immovable and bent about human beings. So of*
> *course they failed. And they will continue to fail*
> *unless the new knowledge about our true makeup is*
> *integrated more fully into the world of public policy,*
> *unless the enchanted story is told along with the*
> *prosaic one. (2011, pp. xiv–xv)*

To tie these two threads of thought together: We need more truly modern humans, in Jung's terms. And to get there, we need more individuals who have made the courageous choice to turn inwards and explore the enchanted story within and who have taken the journey to wholeness within themselves and are therefore able to call forth more wholeness in the world around us. To get there, we need more individuals willing to turn their attention to the blind spot and to take seriously the urgency of developing at the innermost Be level of the Flame. Equally important, we need more individuals, organizations, communities, and nations with a capacity to effectively invite more of us into this journey and guide us skillfully along the well-worn yet still mysterious path of inner development that leads to greater wholeness and higher consciousness.

Once again, my deepest hope is that the ideas presented here serve to move us in that direction in the years ahead.

6

THE POWER OF FINDING THE
RIGHT QUESTION

*To ask the right question is already half the solution
to a problem. – Carl Jung (1981, p. 23)*

The city of Lawrence is a working-class community in
northeastern Massachusetts, about 45 minutes north of Boston. The city has been nicknamed the "Immigrant City" due
to the fact that wave after wave of immigrants settled there
from the late 1800s onwards, attracted by its strong
manufacturing base and affordable housing (Cole, 2002). In
modern times – since the 1960s – the city has seen an influx of
immigrant families from Puerto Rico, the Dominican Republic, and Vietnam.

In 1988, Dan Rothstein was a newly minted Doctor of
Education from Harvard working in the Department of
Community Development in Lawrence. The city had received
a grant from the Annie E. Casey foundation to work with
local parents on a dropout prevention initiative, and Dan was
leading that effort. Early in the process, he recruited a
particularly active and engaged local parent, Luz Santana, to
be a partner in moving the work forward. It was the beginning

of a professional collaboration that is still going strong more than 30 years later.

Dan and Luz were working with parents of students who were academically at risk of dropping out of school, trying to understand why the parents were not more engaged with the school system. Many of these parents were immigrants for whom English was a second language, and they found it intimidating to simply interact with the school system, never mind advocate for their children. In conversations with these parents, one theme kept recurring again and again as a barrier to more engagement: *They didn't know what questions to ask.*

Parent after parent made it clear that they were reluctant to meet with school administrators because they didn't know what they would ask if they were to find themselves face-to-face with a representative of the system charged with educating their kids.

Luz and Dan's first response was to attempt to solve this problem in the simplest way possible: Give the parents a list of questions to ask. It didn't take long for the limitations of that approach to become apparent. Parents would have an initial meeting with school staff, and would then return to Luz and Dan and say, "OK….what do I do next?" It was clear that simply giving parents a set of questions was not an empowering and sustainable approach; it actually recreated a sense of dependency among the parents, who seemed to be learning the lesson that they needed direction from others before they could play a more active role in supporting their children.

Luz and Dan realized that they had to try a different approach. Rather than hand out a list of questions, they had to find a way to help these parents *formulate their own questions in order to find the right questions to ask on their own.* They got to work on developing a process to do just that, and from their early experiments quickly saw the potential in the approach. When individuals learned how to find the right questions to ask to advocate for things they cared about, they were able to move out of a state of fear, passivity, and dependence and start showing up for their kids. They gained the confidence to engage with the systems that impacted their lives; equally important, they could continue to engage by finding the right questions to ask after their first set of questions were answered.

It was powerful stuff, and Dan and Luz have spent the last four decades of their lives refining and disseminating this work. They created a nonprofit called the Right Question Institute (RQI) (www.rightquestion.org) and have deployed the methodology in a variety of sectors, from healthcare to social services to education to voter engagement. As of this writing, they've published two books (a third is on the way), and their work on question formulation has been written up in Forbes, the New York Times, the Atlantic, and more (2011, 2016). In recent years, they have begun to frame their work as an approach to what they call "Microdemocracy," which they define as "the idea that ordinary encounters with public agencies are opportunities for individual citizens to 'act democratically' and participate effectively in decisions that affect them" (The Right Question Institute, 2021). The idea is that democracy is strengthened when people feel empowered to engage skillfully with the organizations and systems they encounter in their daily lives.

As you may recall from Chapter 2, I first crossed paths with Dan when I was struggling to find a powerful way to help City Year AmeriCorps members develop meaningful topics to bring into the Idealist's Journey reflection spaces. We had learned that simply creating a space for reflection was not enough; if participants spent the time discussing trivialities or having conversations that felt unfocused and lacking in a clear purpose, they felt – justifiably – that these spaces were a waste of time. Even worse, these unfocused conversations could easily devolve into a space for venting frustrations and sharing complaints. When that happened, these sessions were worse than a waste of time; they became actively negative experiences that served to undermine idealism, corrode morale, and allow a toxic culture to take root in the organization. On the other hand, in cases where conversations felt focused, purposeful, and highly relevant to actual challenges that AmeriCorps members were confronting in their service, participants found these spaces to be both valuable and productive. They actively looked forward to these sessions and would ask for more time to continue conversations that felt so useful.

The problem was that I couldn't figure out how to make sure AmeriCorps members consistently brought topics to these sessions that were clear, personally meaningful, and power-fully presented. It turns out that sifting through all of the complexity that AmeriCorps members encountered through their work in schools to discern what was really most strategic and compelling to bring to reflection discussions was not an easy task. Simply asking participants to talk about something important wasn't effective. Participants often showed up with their first hot take regarding an issue that was on their mind; minutes into the discussion it would become clear that they had just scratched the surface of some deeper matter, and the discussion ended up becoming more of a search for the real underlying issue than a focused exploration of some clearly articulated matter. Or, participants would try to guess a topic that they thought their peers would want to discuss rather than turn inwards to connect with something that mattered deeply to themselves. In these cases, it turned out that more often than not those guesses were off base, resulting in con-versations where literally nobody in the group really cared much about the issue on the table.

In time, I came to realize that this challenge was another example of the deep interconnection between the innermost way of being of the presenter and the outer-world experience of individuals in relationship with that individual. In cases where AmeriCorps members achieved inner clarity about an issue they cared about and felt deeply connected to why that issue was important, then the group conversation about that issue was focused, meaningful, and productive. If the AmeriCorps member had not yet figured out the essence of the issue they wanted to discuss, then the group conversation felt aimless, unfocused, and of questionable value to the presenter and the group as a whole. The more of these sessions that I observed, the more apparent it became that in these spaces, AmeriCorps members were "calling forth" discussions that mirrored their inner state of clarity or confusion.

How, then, do you support an individual to achieve powerful inner clarity regarding the question or issue they want to bring to a group to discuss? Equally important: How do you make that happen consistently and at scale, so that week after week, hundreds of individuals will show up for these sessions having achieved that inner clarity?

While we had experimented with some structures and processes that were somewhat helpful in addressing this challenge, it was clear that we had not really figured this out. And we surely did not have anything close to a highly sophisticated, cutting-edge approach to this work that represented the leading edge of innovation in this area.

That's when I crossed paths with Dan and Luz.

As I had previously shared, Dan and I met when we both participated in the Boston cohort of a Jewish leadership development program called Selah. There were about 15 participants in that program, and we met multiple times over the course of a year. During our first session, Dan told me a bit about his work as co-founder of the RQI. He explained to me that he and his colleague Luz had found a way to help people formulate their own questions, and I was intrigued but also mystified. I loved the concepts that he was discussing – and could sense immediately the potential relevance to the challenges we were struggling with around reflection – but had no clue what it actually looked like to help individuals formulate their own questions.

Fortunately, Dan was excited to share his model with City Year AmeriCorps members, and I was eager to see how this approach worked. We agreed to try a "Question Formulation" pilot at City Year New Hampshire and set a date for Dan and Luz to do a training with some AmeriCorps members there. I made sure to be present to experience this model myself and see how the training was received.

What Dan and Luz shared that day was a five-step process called the Question Formulation Technique (QFT) that could be easily displayed on a single PowerPoint slide. It's simple enough for young children to understand, yet it has proven to be the most sophisticated and effective framework I have ever encountered for helping individuals engage with the full complexity of their experiences and emerge with clear, powerful questions that illuminate personally meaningful challenges in profound ways. I made two small tweaks to the model (I'll explain more about this below) and then built it into the Idealist's Journey model for the entire organization the next year. It quickly became an integral element of the reflection work at City Year, and now in the work we are doing at the New Politics Leadership Academy with aspiring politicians. After working with it for over a decade, I remain amazed at what this deceptively simple process makes possible for individuals and how strategic it can be for organizations seeking to empower everyone from the C-Suite to front-line staff to more effectively engage with complexity.

Because this work is so central to this model of a scalable approach to inner development, I've decided to present the QFT in detail in this chapter. If you are interested in gaining a deeper understanding of what this process is, how it works, and why it is so powerful, I invite you to read on. If you are not currently interested in this level of detail, feel free to skim this chapter or simply move on to Chapter 7.

THE QUESTION FORMULATION TECHNIQUE

After decades of developing this model, the folks at the RQI have refined this process down to five steps. Here they are:

1. Develop a Question Focus

2. Produce Your Questions

3. Improve Your Questions

4. Prioritize Your Questions

5. Reflect

Here's a deeper dive into how each step works and why it matters:

Step 1: Develop a Question Focus

A "QFocus" is a statement that is generated by an educator or trainer that provides a focus for all the steps that follow. This statement should meet the following standards:

- It is brief and simply stated.

- It is NOT a question.

- It provokes and stimulates new lines of thinking.

In their book *Make Just One Change: Teach Students to Ask Their Own Questions*, they offer the following examples of QFocuses that teachers might offer to students:

The Inside of a Cell

Defeating Math Anxiety

Pollution harms Boston residents (2011, p. 31)

The idea here is that educators bring this kind of focused statement to the group, and the group then generates questions related to this statement. The idea is simple but powerful: Instead of providing answers or sharing information, educators invite students to connect with their own questions related to the issue highlighted by the QFocus. It's an approach that is explained in detail in *Make Just One Change*, and more than 300,000 educators have been trained in this model to date.

While I honor the value of this method, I immediately struggled with its limitations for the type of leadership development experience we were trying to create for our AmeriCorps members. I suppose that we could have always had the Idealist's Journey facilitator come up with a QFocus for the group, but what if somebody in the group had something else on their mind that they wanted to explore?

At stake in this decision was a vital matter with profound importance to the work of leadership development: *Who gets to decide what aspect of reality deserves my attention?* In many matters related to the "DO" and "KNOW" level of the Flame, it was appropriate to treat AmeriCorps members as novices who needed to be taught the latest theories and trained in best practices. There were experts who had spent years exploring, say, behavior management or literacy tutoring, and it was strategic to train AmeriCorps members in the kinds of proven best practices that would strengthen their work with students and help them avoid months of using ineffective tactics. Those spaces were about horizontal development, in which AmeriCorps members gained new knowledge and skills. The Idealist's Journey was not a traditional training space, however. It was designed to invite participants to connect with the deeply personal meaning of their experiences. In this space, it was important that every participant had the opportunity to decide for themselves the issues that they found most personally important and compelling. These spaces were about vertical development and earning a "bigger mind" rather than gaining new knowledge and skills.

For these reasons, we chose to take a different path for this first step in the process. Rather than having an educator or facilitator come up with a QFocus to which others would respond, we empowered every AmeriCorps member to select for themselves the issue that would serve as the focus for this question finding process. Inspired by the Flame metaphor that was so central to this work, we decided to call this opening statement a "Spark" rather than a "QFocus." Our primary guidance to participants as they select a Spark is to find something that "gets them in the gut." The most important criteria here is that they connect with an issue that really matters to them.

This decision to allow every participant to choose their own focus – their own Spark – may seem like a minor change, but it represents a powerful response to the context in which leadership development occurs today. In years past – when the context was more hierarchical and less interdependent – there was less of a need for front-line staff to find their own way forward in the face of complexity. In most organizations, the work of engaging with complexity was done by folks at the top. It was up to individuals in the C-suites to grapple with changes in the marketplace, competitive threats, and new opportunities. This relatively small group of individuals would think it all through, decide on a strategy, and then provide direction to middle managers who would make sure front-line staff were executing on the plans created by those at the top. In this arrangement, the only individuals who were expected to grapple with complexity were those most senior leaders; everyone else could just focus on doing what they were told.

In the new context of a more interconnected and interdependent network, this arrangement no longer works. By virtue of their position at the front lines and grassroots, front line staff often encounter challenges and opportunities that senior leaders are too removed from the action to see. And the environment at every level is so complex that everyone everywhere in the organization is confronted with the struggle to find their way forward in the face of complexity. To be sure, the complexity encountered by senior leaders charged with leading a multi-million dollar nonprofit is different from the complexity encountered by AmeriCorps members charged with tutoring a group of middle school students on the front lines of this work. But both contexts are wildly complex in their own way and can be best addressed by individuals who can effectively discern what matters most in all that complexity and find their way forward.

This, then, is the power of crafting a Spark. In this process, individuals at every level are trusted to decide for themselves which aspects of their reality merit more attention. It's a deeply empowering opportunity, and it requires an understanding by folks at the top that there are limits to their ability to provide direction and control to everyone in the organization. If an organization wants to support staff in building their skills at confronting complexity, then the organization must create spaces in which individuals are trusted to decide for themselves what elements of their experience merit attention and focus. Once they have a chance to select an issue that is truly alive for them, they need space to discuss and explore that issue in thoughtful and productive ways with colleagues.

To give you a sense of what crafting a Spark looked like in the City Year context, here are some Sparks developed by AmeriCorps members over the years:

- My student doesn't believe he can succeed in school.
- We just learned that my school will be shut down by the district next year.
- A year of national service is not yet a civic rite of passage for all Americans.
- My student is struggling because his older brother just got arrested and sent to jail.

And here are a few Sparks generated by participants in New Politics Leadership Academy programs (these are military veterans or national service alumni wondering if they should serve through electoral politics):

- I dislike the idea of campaigning and feel it could be exhausting/unsustainable for my personality.
- People will think I'm a bad mother for spending that much time away from home.
- I don't have the right experience or expertise to make a meaningful difference as a politician.
- The complexity of issues to tackle while having limited experience is scary.

As you can see, right from the start this process challenges individuals to get clear about something going on in their world that is personally important. Already, we have achieved a level of clarity and meaning that is far beyond what we were able to consistently generate with any other process we tried to help individuals develop their presentations for these reflection discussions. And we're just getting started with the QFT!

Step 2: Produce Questions

Once a Spark Statement has been selected, the next step is to brainstorm a set of questions related to the Spark. The task here is to quickly generate a list of questions using the following "Rules for Producing Questions":

- Ask as many questions as you can.

- Do not stop to discuss, judge, or answer any question.

- Write down every question exactly as it is stated.

- Change any statement into a question ((2011, p. 43).

This task is best done in a small group of 3–4 individuals, as hearing questions offered by others often generates a more diverse and creative thinking at this step.

The goal of this step is to encourage divergent thinking related to the topic at hand. Here's an example of what this looks like in practice, using a Spark that was generated during a New Politics Leadership Academy program.

Spark

I dislike the idea of campaigning and feel it could be exhausting/unsustainable for my personality.

List of Questions

How do candidates take care of themselves while campaigning?

Is the possibility of winning worth it?

How do candidates create boundaries so that campaigns don't take over their entire lives?

Is the commitment required to run for a state level seat different from what is required to run for a federal seat?

What activities are most effective at keeping me resilient?

Are there candidates who have run despite not enjoying the campaigning process?

How might I make campaigning more energizing?

What are best practices in staying healthy during demanding times of life?

Are there other ways I can serve through politics that aren't as exhausting?

Who could I speak to get a useful perspective on this challenge?

What resources exist to support candidates over the course of a campaign?

What lessons learned from past challenges could help you deal with this issue?

Is it possible to become a politician without campaigning?

How do I balance my own need for comfort with the need to serve others at this critical time?

What issues do I care about enough to make this sacrifice worth it?

As you can see, this list provides a host of different ways to explore the issue highlighted in the Spark. Any one of these questions has the potential to lead to a rich and productive discussion that could provide useful information and insights to the individual who created the Spark that launched this question generation process. By creating this list without spending any time or energy on discussion or debating any specific question, individuals are challenged to consider a wide array of perspectives on the issue that almost certainly push their thinking in new directions.

One of my favorite facts about this process that I often mention at this step is this: After training literally hundreds of thousands of individuals in this work, the staff at the RQI have found that *on average, individuals end up choosing the* **thirteenth** *question generated as the question they want to use for their presentation.*

Think about that for a moment and consider your process when trying to think through something important. How often do you quickly jump to a particular perspective or approach to that issue and just run with it? How often do you pause to question that initial approach and consider an alternative? And how often do you *repeat that process 12 times?* The answer for most of us, I assume it is safe to say, is never. This is the power of the QFT: By pushing us to think divergently and generate a bunch of questions, we are compelled to break out of default ways of thinking that may be limited or ineffective and explore a wealth of other perspectives. Frequently, it's not the second or fourth or even the sixth perspective that unlocks something crucial for us, but the thirteenth. But you'll only discover that if you generate those second or fourth or sixth possibilities, and still keep going in your efforts to think divergently about the task at hand.

Step 3: Improve the Questions

Once this list of questions has been created, the next step is to "improve" the questions, an effort that has a very specific and technical meaning in this process. "Improving" the questions means turning any close-ended questions that could be quickly answered with a simple "yes or no" into open-ended questions that invite deeper inquiry. It's important to note that this is NOT about analyzing the substance of every question to assess its quality in some intellectual sense. Rather, this is simply about making sure that every question on the list is open-ended.

Here's what this step looks like with the list we just encountered in Step 2. The close-ended questions on the list appear with strike-through text, and newly worded versions of those questions appear right below highlighted in gray (all the other questions were already open-ended and did not need to be changed).

Spark

I dislike the idea of campaigning and feel it could be exhausting/unsustainable for my personality.

List of Questions

How do candidates take care of themselves while campaigning?

~~Is the possibility of winning worth it?~~

What aspects of campaigning would make it worth it to endure the potential exhaustion?

How do candidates create boundaries so that campaigns don't take over their entire lives?

~~Is the commitment required to run for a state level seat different from what is required to run for a federal seat?~~

How is the commitment required to run at the state level different from the commitment required to run at the federal level?

What activities are most effective at keeping me resilient?

~~Are there candidates who have run despite not enjoying the campaigning process?~~

Which candidates have run for office despite not enjoying the campaign process?

How might I make campaigning more energizing?

What are best practices in staying healthy during demanding times of life?

~~Are there other ways I can serve through politics that aren't as exhausting?~~

How else might I serve through politics that might be more sustainable?

Who could I speak to get a useful perspective on this challenge?

What resources exist to support candidates over the course of a campaign?

What lessons learned from past challenges could help you deal with this issue?

~~Is it possible to become a politician without campaigning?~~

How might I become a politician without campaigning?

How do I balance my own need for comfort with the need to serve others at this critical time?

What issues do I care about enough to make this sacrifice worth it?

As you can see, there were five questions from the original list that were phrased in close-ended language. In each case, a new question was created that stays true to the spirit of the original question but uses open-ended language. Now that we've gone through the list and made these changes, we find ourselves with a list of all open-ended questions.

According to RQI, the key insight here is this: "The construction and phrasing of a question shapes the kind of information you can expect to receive" (2011, p. 85). A close-ended "yes or no" question evokes a debate; an open-ended question evokes a dialogue. If our goal is to invite groups to engage in deep inquiry about issues that matter to a member of the group, offering an open-ended question to get the discussion started is a powerful tool.

Step 4: Prioritize Your Questions

At this point, we have selected an issue that is personally meaningful, engaging in divergent thinking by generating a list of questions, and then made sure that all the questions open-ended. It is now time to begin the process of deciding which of these questions will be used for the Spark Session Presentation.

This involves a process of prioritizing the questions based on which questions are most compelling to the individual who generated the original Spark. This is not about assessing which questions are articulated in the most elegant way or are in some sense the most intellectually sophisticated; rather, this is about exploring which questions are most alive and energizing for the presenter.

Once again, we encourage that individual to use one simple yet powerful criteria when prioritizing their questions: Go with the question that "gets you in the gut." Shift out of the mode of intellect and analysis and start paying attention to the wisdom of your body. This isn't about selecting the question that your brain thinks you should choose; it's about sensing the question that evokes a gut response because of how important and alive that question feels to you as a whole human being. We instruct people to first pick the three questions that stand out as most intriguing; then, from that subset of three, pick the *one question* that resonates most powerfully and is likely to generate a discussion that you would really like to have with your fellow group members.

This is another seemingly simple approach that is grounded in a powerful response to the context in which leadership occurs today. Once again, we are extending a deep level of trust to individuals by empowering them to choose for themselves how they most want to explore an issue they find personally compelling. It's important to note that different people are likely to prioritize the same list of questions in quite different ways. This process is not grounded in a belief that there is some objectively "best" question that can be discerned through reason and analysis. Rather, it is based on an understanding that each of us approaches personally meaningful issues in different ways, and for the purposes of this work, the right question to bring to a group for a discussion is a question that really matters to whoever selected the Spark in the first place.

Here's how this step works using the list we've been working with for the last couple steps. The individual who generated the Spark takes a look at the full list of questions, and places three stars next to the three questions that stand out as most compelling.

Spark

I dislike the idea of campaigning and feel it could be
  exhausting/unsustainable for my personality.

List of Questions

***How do candidates take care of themselves while
  campaigning?

~~Is the possibility of winning worth it?~~

What aspects of campaigning would make it worth it to endure the potential exhaustion?

How do candidates create boundaries so that campaigns don't take over their entire lives?

~~Is the commitment required to run for a state-level seat different from what is required to run for a federal seat?~~

How is the commitment required to run at the state level different from the commitment required to run at the federal level?

What activities are most effective at keeping me resilient?

~~Are there candidates who have run despite not enjoying the campaigning process?~~

Which candidates have run for office despite not enjoying the campaign process?

How might I make campaigning more energizing?

What are best practices in staying healthy during demanding times of life?

~~Are there other ways I can serve through politics that aren't as exhausting?~~

How else might I serve through politics that might be more sustainable?

Who could I speak to get at useful perspective on this challenge?

***What resources exist to support candidates over the course of a campaign?

What lessons learned from past challenges could help you deal with this issue?

~~Is it possible to become a politician without campaigning?~~

How might I become a politician without campaigning?

***How do I balance my own need for comfort with the need to serve others at this critical time?

What issues do I care about enough to make this sacrifice worth it?

Here's the list of three questions that the individual selected:

***How do candidates take care of themselves while campaigning?

***What resources exist to support candidates over the course of a campaign?

***How do I balance my own need for comfort with the need to serve others at this critical time?

After careful consideration of these three possibilities, the individual decides that the question that most clearly "gets her in the gut" is the third of these three questions: "How do I balance my own need for comfort with the need to serve others at this critical time?" This, then, is the question that will be integrated in the final Spark Session Presentation.

As this is often done in small groups, we make it clear that the task of the other members of the group at this stage of the process is to help the individual selecting the question attain inner clarity. It's not appropriate to advocate for a particular question that you think is intriguing; the focus should be on asking questions and providing feedback to help Spark creator get clear. Questions like "Why do you like that question?" and feedback like "You seem really energized by the first question, but a bit more ambivalent when you talk about the second question" are what we are looking for here. This should not be an argument about which question is truly the best; it should be a dialogue in which others help the Spark Creator find the question that they personally care about most.

Step 5: Reflect

At this step, we arrive again at a place where we decided to make a tweak to the QFT. In the process as it is presented by the RQI, this is the step where a group dives into a dialogue focused on reflecting on the questions that emerged in Step 4. Since the QFT is usually done in classrooms where a teacher has provided a QFocus for the class, it makes sense to dive into reflection at this point in the process. Since we use the process to help individuals prepare for a conversation that will happen at some point in the future, we tweaked this step as follows.

Step 5: Craft the Spark Session Presentation

For this final step of the process, this involves combining the Spark Statement that was created in Step #1 with the question that emerged from the prioritization exercise in Step #4. When presented together, these become the Spark Session Presentation. In this case, here's how this looks:

> *I dislike the idea of campaigning and feel it could be exhausting/unsustainable for my personality. How do I balance my own need for comfort with the need to serve others at this critical time?*

As you can see, this is a very concise, clear statement that usually only takes 10–15 seconds to share with a group. It focuses the group on an issue that is personally meaningful to the person who is bringing the issue to the space, and it provides a clear question that invites the group to begin exploring that issue from a perspective that is also deeply meaningful to the person sharing this with the group.

Here are a few other Spark Session Presentations taken from participants in programming created by the New Politics Leadership Academy:

> *People will think I'm a bad mother for spending that much time away from home. What change can I create for my daughters?*

> *I don't have the right experience or expertise to make a meaningful difference as a politician. Who am I to make a difference as a politician?*

> *The complexity of issues to tackle while having little experience is scary. How much experience do I need to effectively lead well?*

> *I don't feel I can forge the right network or coalition to propel a campaign. What connections are most effective in supporting a run for office?*

At this point, the process is complete, and individuals have arrived at a Spark Session Presentation that they can bring to their group to kick off a conversation focused on reflection, dialogue, and learning.

As you'll recall, the key challenge that we were facing with the reflection work was that we couldn't find a way to support participants in showing up with clear and mean-ingful questions that consistently generated productive dialogue. Looking at the Spark Session Presentations listed above, I hope the reader can see how this QFT powerfully solves that problem. These presentations are not trivialities that would be a waste of time to discuss nor are they vaguely articulated questions presented in a rambling fashion that leaves everybody wondering what to talk about. With the introduction of the QFT, we found a way to ensure that nearly every group nearly every time was able to jump immediately into a focused, engaging conversation about something that mattered a great deal. It was a game changing discovery, and it was the missing piece that allowed us to take this approach to scalable reflection from good to great.

QUESTION FORMULATION, PIXAR, AND BRAINTRUSTS

In his book *Creativity Inc: Overcoming the Unseen Forces That Stand in the Way of True Inspiration*, President of Pixar Animation Ed Catmull explains how he built an organization that was able to produce an unrivaled string of hit movies like *Toy Story, Wall-E, Finding Dory, Cars* and many more (2014). Among the many best practices shared in the book, Catmull explains that a gathering he calls "the Braintrust" is one of the most important. At Pixar, a Braintrust is a group of skilled storytellers who gather regularly. The director of a film in production comes to the group with questions or challenges he or she is currently confronting, and the members of the group offer their candid and honest thoughts about how to solve the problem. The director emerges having encountered multiple perspectives on how to solve the storytelling problem they brought to the group and is empowered to decide how best to use all the feedback.

Catmull explains that a key reason the Braintrust is effective is because it has no authority. He explains it like this:

> *The director does not have to follow any of the*
> *specific suggestions given. After a Braintrust meeting,*
> *it is up to him or her to figure out how to address the*
> *feedback…We believe that ideas – and thus, films –*
> *only become great when they are challenged and*
> *tested. In academia, peer review is the process by*
> *which professors are evaluated by others in their*
> *field. I like to think of the Braintrust as Pixar's*
> *version of peer review, a forum that ensures we raise*
> *our game – not by being prescriptive but by offering*
> *candor and deep analysis (2014, p. 93).*

Of course, not every organization is crafting stories that become major Hollywood movies. Organizations are focused on many other missions and are full of individuals with experience and expertise in advancing those missions. The QFT combined with the Journey framework effectively creates an ecology of Braintrusts across an organization. In the case of City Year, all the AmeriCorps members were committed idealists spending their days in schools supporting students; when a member of the group shares a question related to that work, the other members of the group surely have highly relevant experience and insights to push the Presenters thinking in productive directions. The same is true at any organization, where multiple individuals with diverse areas of expertise and experience are working together on a shared goal. Inevitably, not every bit of advice offered is going to be useful, and not every conversation will produce breakthrough insights, but in general, we can trust that individuals emerge from these sessions feeling that their thinking has been pushed, deepened, and expanded in productive ways.

Again, these spaces are designed to promote vertical development. In these conversations, every member of the group is challenged to engage with different perspectives, consider different ways of understanding issues, and have their default beliefs and assumptions surfaced and challenged. The fact that these sessions are not intended to arrive at a shared agreement on a "correct" answer and clear path forward is a feature, not a bug. These opportunities to spend time in spaces of curiosity, inquiry, dialogue and reflection helps individuals to grow "bigger minds" in ways that build the organization's capacity to navigate complexity at all levels.

I hope it is clear that this approach is applicable to any other context one can imagine, despite the fact that the examples presented here are drawn from my organizational experiences. One of the remarkable things about the QFT is that it does not require that program designers or facilitators possess industry- or sector-specific knowledge or expertise. In the case of the organizations where I have worked, it freed both HQ staff (in this case, me), as well as the hundreds of group facilitators spread across the organization from having to guess what content would be most helpful to participants to discuss. This is a good thing because it is an act of hubris to believe that individuals higher-up in the hierarchy will always know best what others in the organization should be thinking about. In fact, once these discussions begin happening across an organization, they become a window into what is occurring in the inner lives of people across the organization. There's no need to guess whether people are feeling exhausted, irritated, confused, or engaged; these discussions offer insights into where people are at, surfacing issues that can be addressed in productive ways long before they fester into urgent crises that explode as if out of nowhere.

Most strategically, the QFT dramatically strengthens the ability of participants to move forward effectively and confidently in the face of complexity. In our programming at the New Politics Leadership Academy, program graduates frequently say something like this: "I used to feel completely overwhelmed by the thought of running for office; now I feel confident that I can figure out my next steps along the way and make it happen!"

It is hard to overstate how valuable and strategic it is to move people from a state of feeling lost and overwhelmed to a sense that they can find their way forward in the face of complex challenges. When everyone at every level of an organization has this capacity to respond skillfully to complexity, they are no longer dependent on senior leaders to have all the answers. They are able to find their own way forward with new levels of confidence and insight, greatly enhancing the organization's capacity to confront complexity.

FINAL THOUGHTS

It's relevant to note that this QFT was originally developed to help marginalized communities step up to advocate more powerfully for themselves in their communities, and in the work presented here, it is currently proving effective at supporting American citizens to step up in one of the most courageous and impactful ways possible. The servant leaders in the programs run by the New Politics Leadership Academy are contemplating running for elected office in one of the most toxic and partisan political environments in American history. Again and again, individuals emerge from our programs saying that this chance to get clear about their questions and think through these issues with thoughtful peers helped them get to a place where they were willing and able to step up in this way.

Few situations require the same level of courage, commitment, and sacrifice as running for office. For many individuals, stepping up to new levels of leadership will mean having courageous conversations at work or at home, taking on a challenging new initiative, or embarking on some new adventure that is scary and uncertain. Wherever we may find ourselves and whatever we may be doing, there are opportunities to step up and lead with more courage, integrity and impact. If we are in need of approaches that are effective at getting people to step up in this way, this approach has been tested in some of the most intense and challenging contexts imaginable.

As we bring this chapter to a close, I'll reemphasize that the approach presented here represents a relatively brief explanation of an adapted version of the powerful work developed by the RQI. Any readers interested in gaining a deeper understanding of their QFT and how it has been implemented by RQI in contexts as diverse as education, social services, healthcare, voter engagement and more are encouraged to check out RQI online at www.rightquestion.org. I also encourage readers to check out the two books published by Dan and Luz: *Make Just One Change: Teach Students to Ask Their Own Questions*, and *Partnering with Parents to Ask the Right Questions*.

7

THE FLAME, THE JOURNEY, AND THE QUEST FOR A NEW POLITICS

It is not the critic who counts; not the man who points out how the strong man stumbles, or where the doer of deeds could have done them better. The credit belongs to the man who is actually in the arena, whose face is marred by dust and sweat and blood; who strives valiantly; who errs, who comes short again and again, because there is no effort without error and shortcoming; but who does actually strive to do the deeds; who knows great enthusiasms, the great devotions; who spends himself in a worthy cause; who at the best knows in the end the triumph of high achievement, and who at the worst, if he fails, at least fails while daring greatly, so that his place shall never be with those cold and timid souls who neither know victory nor defeat. – Teddy Roosevelt (1910)

It's the first session of a program called "Answering the Call (ATC)," and a diverse group of individuals are gathered on a Zoom call engaged in a discussion on their Personal

Leadership Mission Statements. One participant is an evangelical Christian military vet from the Midwest; another is a trans woman who was a former Marine; another is a Black male educator and Teach for America alum, another is a white female Returned Peace Corps volunteer currently working in a small community nonprofit, and the final participant is a white male Air Force vet currently working in the corporate world. Although political affiliation was never directly discussed, it is clear that some of these participants have conservative views while others are highly progressive. At this session, they engage in a substantive and respectful conversation about the challenges of crafting a clear personal leadership mission and living with integrity to that mission.

In the highly polarized culture of America today, it is rare for these individuals to cross paths; it is rarer still for them to engage in respectful and productive dialogue. Yet these conversations happen consistently at the New Politics Leadership Academy (NPLA), where this Flame and Journey work is central to the organization's approach to leadership development.

The mission of the NPLA is to revitalize American democracy by recruiting and developing servant leaders who put country and community over self. These are individuals who have demonstrated through their life choices that they are dedicated to serving others. They have spent years either on the front lines or at the grassroots working alongside fellow Americans with different backgrounds and beliefs to achieve a shared mission. They are idealistic and principled but also pragmatic and grounded in the reality of how change actually happens. They understand in a deeply personal way how decisions made at the federal level impact the experiences of soldiers in battle, teachers in classrooms, or communities in the developing world.

There are millions of these individuals currently serving in a myriad of ways in communities across the nation. However, only a tiny sliver currently choose to serve through politics. Although the reasons for that are complex, the impact is clear: Too many of our politicians are driven by hungers for power, attention, love, or greed; not enough are in office as a next step in a lifetime commitment to serve others.

NPLA is trying to revitalize our politics by bringing more proven, tested servant leaders into elected office. It's an organization seeking to develop servant leaders at scale in one of the most challenging contexts imaginable: American politics today. And the Flame and Journey model we've been exploring is central to this effort.

In this chapter, we'll briefly discuss the background and history of this organization, and we'll explore what it looks like when the Flame and Journey approach is made central to an organization from the very beginning.

THE NEW POLITICS STORY

New Politics was founded in 2015 by Emily Cherniack, a lifelong servant leader who understood how challenging it was to make the transition from service to politics. Emily started her career at City Year, first as an AmeriCorps member and then as a staff member. She spent her days in a school in Boston running afterschool programming, vacation camps, and other youth development programming. The days were long and exhausting, but Emily loved it. She came to view herself as a youth worker and a "service person" who found meaning and purpose by providing direct service at the grass roots in the world of education.

Later, she found herself pulled into politics when her mentor, City Year co-founder Alan Khazei, decided to run for Senate in Massachusetts in 2009. She became Alan's Deputy Finance Director and for the first time encountered the world of electoral politics. Emily often references the movie *The Matrix* when she talks about these experiences in politics, saying that stepping into the political world was "like taking the red pill and suddenly finding myself in an entirely new reality." Emily quickly realized that the political space was opaque, counterintuitive, and full of dark forces and ego-driven players. The contrast between her experiences in the service movement could not have been more stark.

Emily emerged from this experience in politics with a commitment to create an organization that would bring more servant leaders into politics. She knew from experience that many of the individuals who serve through the military or national service learn to operate with humility and courage. They learn how to work as part of diverse teams to achieve a mission, and they know what it means to serve a cause larger than self. All of those skills and capacities are extremely relevant to politics, but currently so many of the individuals who choose to seek elected office lack this experience. She knew she wanted that to change.

Equally important, Emily had encountered many political candidates who quickly learned the technical skills of running for office (for example, how to knock on doors or how to get lawn signs printed) but could not powerfully articulate their own "why" for running for office. Every time these candidates spoke, voters could sense that lack of clarity and connection to some deep inner sense of purpose. Emily knew how to support and train candidates on the technical details, but figuring out how to help candidates do the inner work to truly know who they were and why they were running was a different challenge. Figuring out how to guide large numbers of servant leaders through that kind of inner work at scale was also part of her vision.

Emily knew about the Flame and Journey work that I had developed at City Year and thought that the approach was a missing element in standard approaches to training candidates. She also thought that inviting people to get clear about their sense of calling could be an effective approach to recruiting more servant leaders to run for elected office. I agreed and was excited to collaborate. We decided to run a pilot program in early 2016.

The program would be an adaptation of the Idealist's Journey experience, tailored to this particular purpose. It would be a four-session small-group reflection experience that combined a workbook presenting a sequence of personal reflection exercises and use of the Question Formulation Technique, and it would be open to individuals with either a military or national service background. We decided to name it "Answering the Call," as the central focus of the experience would be exploring the question of whether participants felt a calling in their soul to seek political office.

To our surprise, 60 people applied for the pilot, and we selected 28. The diversity of backgrounds and experiences in that group was notable; among the participants were some 23-year-olds who had just completed a year with AmeriCorps and mid-career elite military vets with multiple advanced degrees. And although we did not formally ask for party affiliation, it became clear over the course of discussions that the group included Democrats, Republicans, and individuals who weren't quite sure which party they aligned with most closely. The sessions occurred during the month of February 2016, and attendance was above 90% for all four sessions.

The evaluation results were extremely positive: 100% of participants felt that the experience was effective in helping them to achieve a new level of personal clarity about their interest in politics as a next step in their journey, and 95% felt that the program was effective at building a pipeline of service program alumni that have engaged seriously with the question of whether they feel personally called to pursue public service. Despite the diversity of service backgrounds and the disparities in age and experience, participants said they felt a remarkable sense of connection to the group based on the shared commitment to service. When asked how the program could be improved, the most frequent response was "make it longer."

If the question was whether the Flame and Journey approach could be used to help servant leaders connect with purpose and get clear within themselves about whether they felt called to step up to enter the toxic, partisan world of politics, the answer was clearly "Yes." Based on the success of the pilot, Emily asked me to make the leap to become the first full-time employee of the NPLA, a non-partisan nonprofit that would be focused on scaling up this approach to leadership development to vastly expand the pipeline of servant leaders seeking elected office. In August 2016, I left my role at City Year to become the Chief Program Officer at the NPLA. After years working to develop and advance this work from my role as a mid-level staff at a large organization, I was excited to step into a brand-new start-up organization as a Senior Leader and help launch an organization founded on this approach to leadership development.

SCALING UP SERVANT LEADERSHIP DEVELOPMENT AS A START-UP ORGANIZATION

During my 10 years at City Year, I was operating as an "intra-preneur" working to create change inside a well-established large-scale organization. That organization had thousands of full-time staff along with thousands of full-time AmeriCorps members. At the risk of understatement, NPLA was a new and different challenge. In those early days, the entire staff of NPLA consisted of Emily and me sitting across a table in a rented office space, figuring out how to build a large-scale servant leadership development from scratch.

Following the success of the ATC pilot, we wasted no time in moving forward with a scale pilot that would involve running four groups in the fall of 2016. This would give us a chance to pilot recruiting and training a small group of ATC facilitators who could successfully implement the program with excellence. That first scale pilot included groups in Boston, New York, LA, and one virtual program. Over the course of my time at City Year I had refined an approach to facilitator training, so this effort was once again about adapting a proven approach to powerfully advance the goals of this new program at the NPLA.

We soon learned that we could recruit and train skilled facilitators who were willing to volunteer their time to lead ATC programs either virtually or in person in cities across the country. It turns out that there is a vast network of skilled and experienced facilitators across the nation, and many were excited to find a way to use their gifts and passion for facilitation to revitalize our troubled politics. It took some time to build our bench of facilitators, but we eventually trained a diverse group of more than 150 facilitators, many of whom returned to lead ATC multiple times after their first experience with the program. In time, we added staff to handle the administrative and customer service elements of running the program and built the organization to a level where we could graduate hundreds of participants from the program, which we ran twice a year.

As of 2024, we have graduated more than 2,500 servant leaders from our ATC program. In our most recent round of programs, 97% of participants reported that the experience helped them to get more clear about their purpose and their political pathway. Before the start of ATC, we ask participants to complete a pre-session survey with questions related to the content of the program, and we ask the same questions following the completion of the program to assess the change that occurred over the course of ATC. The points below show the results of these pre/post-survey questions:

- **86%** of participants "agree" or "strongly agree" that they are now clear about their leadership mission compared to **74%** who stated they were clear about their leadership mission prior to the start of ATC.

- **83%** of participants "agree" or "strongly agree" that they are clear about their shadow mission at the end of the program compared to the **33%** of participants who stated that they "agree" or "strongly agree" they were clear about their shadow mission before the start of ATC. This 50-percentage point change is the most dramatic shift created by the program and is surely the result of the fact that this concept is new to the majority of participants in the program.

- **84%** of participants feel that they understand what they need to do to get involved in politics from where they are now compared to **39%** before the start of ATC. This 45-percentage point change is also dramatic and suggests that the program is helpful at guiding servant leaders toward greater clarity regarding how to enter politics in a practical sense.

Here are a few examples of what participants have to say about the program:

> *Answering The Call is the perfect program for you if you're unsure of how you fit into the world as a person, and more so as a servant leader.*

> *My experience with Answering the Call made me believe once again in the "I can." It definitely gave me the "push" I have been waiting for years to start serving my community. I feel confident and ready for action.*

> *I feel anyone that served and is thinking of continuing to serve our country being politically active should attend this course. It will help you look in the mirror and understand yourself so you can pick a path that is best for you.*

> *Answering the Call was exactly what I didn't know I needed. It provided me with the time and space to reflect on my service thus far and how I may want to continue that service in the future.*

Clearly, the program is effective at helping participants connect with their own sense of purpose. With this new clarity, they find it easier to discern their own path forward at this time of tremendous complexity. For some of them, they realize that they won't have integrity with themselves if they don't step up to serve in politics. Like soldiers with the courage to run toward the battle, they decide that they need to enter the political arena, no matter how toxic and partisan our politics have become.

Of course, we have gone on to create additional programs that allow graduates of ATC to continue developing in powerful ways. For ATC grads who emerge with clarity that they want to become candidates, we offer a follow-up program called Foundations. For ATC grads that realize they are not interested in being a candidate but want to work as a campaign staffer, we offer a program called Staffing School. We have also developed an ongoing series of programming for alumni who want to stay engaged with politics and connected to this community of fellow servant leaders.

Naturally, each of these follow-up programs includes content that is more tactical. To use the language of the Flame: ATC works primarily at the BE level, and the follow-up programs shift to the KNOW and DO levels of the Flame once individuals have gotten clear on the path that they feel called to pursue. For our purposes here, there is no need to discuss the content of those later courses in more detail. What matters here is that NPLA has implemented the Flame and Journey model in ways that help individuals connect with their own purpose and sense of calling in a manner that is powerful and scalable. Participants begin the program with a lot of uncertainty and doubt; they emerge with a sense of clarity and focus, and a fierce desire to live their purpose with new levels of courage and commitment.

At this point, we know of hundreds who have gone on to run for office at every level from School Board to Congress. To get a sense of who some of the individuals are and where they serve, check out the NPLA website at www.newpoliticsacademy.org.

A full review of the impact that all these servant leaders are having in their communities is beyond the scope of this chapter. My focus here is on the approach we use to develop servant leaders at scale, so for now I'll just say this: The Flame and Journey model has been the foundation of NPLA's programming from the very beginning and is being used to guide a diverse community of individuals through a powerful process of inner development. The evaluation data are clear that our programming helps participants get clear about their mission, their shadow, what they feel called to do with their lives, and how they can effectively move forward with pursuing that call in the face of great complexity. It produces these outcomes consistently, year after year, with hundreds of participants annually. It's a proven, tested, effective approach to developing servant leaders at scale.

IT'S ABOUT PURPOSE, NOT JUST POLITICS

This chapter tells the story about how the Flame and Journey approach has been used at New Politics as an approach to recruiting and developing political leaders. I am grateful for the opportunity to work on leadership development in the realm of politics at this critical moment for our nation and the world. The servant leaders who enroll in our programs are among the most inspiring and courageous individuals I've ever met, and they give me tremendous hope for the future. It is a pleasure and an honor to be part of their journey.

That being said, it is important to step back at this point and remember that the work of cultivating purpose – the work illuminated by the Flame and the Journey – is not fundamentally and exclusively about politics. One of the things that makes our ATC program unique in the landscape of political candidate training programs is how little the curriculum focuses on technical or tactical issues related to running for office. Rather, ATC focuses on guiding individuals through the work at the innermost BE level of the Flame: clarifying our mission, confronting our shadow, discerning what we feel called to do with our lives, and reflecting on what it means to live with integrity to our deepest sense of purpose.

While we are harnessing this approach to invite more servant leaders to run for office, it's important to highlight that none of this inner work is inherently or essentially about electoral politics. This process of reflection and self-discovery is essentially about connecting with one's own sense of purpose, mission, and calling. These are universal and deeply human questions to explore, and this process of reflection and self-discovery is an experience that we all must undertake if we are to find our own unique path of purpose in the world.

At the start of this book, I shared an insight that represents the foundation of the leadership development approach presented here:

> *The work of inner change and the work of outer change are too interconnected to separate; organizations must therefore become skillful at engaging in both outer and inner change in effective and integrated ways.*

As you hopefully now understand, The Flame and the Journey work presented in this book represents a practical approach for organizations seeking to integrate these two dimensions of change in effective ways. The Flame model illuminates the relationship between outer and inner dimensions of change and The Journey provides a proven, tested approach to inviting people into an inner journey and guiding them through a powerful process of self-awareness and self-discovery. Whether we are talking about organizations seeking to adapt to changing realities or citizens coming together to care for their communities, the need to work skillfully with the inner dimensions of change is becoming more and more apparent.

We'll bring this book to a close with an exploration of the emerging movement to make that happen on a global scale.

8

THE INNER DEVELOPMENT GOALS AND THE EMERGENCE OF A GLOBAL MOVEMENT HIGHLIGHTING INNER WORK

When facing challenging tasks, there is a need for a range of cognitive and emotional skills and other qualities that go beyond what most people normally learn in schools and higher education. We believe that significant knowledge and insight has accumulated over the years about what these skills and qualities are and how they evolve, in several research fields, such as adult learning and development and in the study of strategic leadership regarding complex issues, such as sustainability studies. The purpose of the Inner Development Goals project is to draw attention to the need to support development of abilities, skills and other inner qualities for people and organizations involved in efforts to contribute to a more sustainable global society. – Inner Development Goals Report, p. 3

THE INNER DEVELOPMENT GOALS STORY

Back in 2012, leaders and activists from around the world gathered at the Earth Summit in Rio de Janeiro. One of the goals of that gathering was to develop a comprehensive set of goals that powerfully address the economic, political, and environmental challenges of our era. These new goals were designed to build on the success of the Millennial Development Goals (MDGs) that had been launched in 2000 to bring a new level of focus to combatting global poverty. As a result of the MDGs, since the year 1990 more than 1 billion people had been lifted out of extreme poverty and child mortality had been reduced by half (UNDP, 2024).

The Sustainable Development Goals (SDGs) represented an effort to build on that momentum while expanding the focus beyond poverty to issues like gender equality, environmental sustainability, quality education, and more. The goals were developed by an open working group that included representatives from 70 different counties complemented by a participatory public consultation process that included 88 national consultations in nations around the world. All of this input and effort led to the development of a set of 17 SDGs that were formally agreed upon by the United Nations in 2015 (UNDP, 2024). The SDGs include goals like ending poverty and hunger, providing a quality education for all children, reducing inequality, and more.

Building on the lessons learned from the MDGs , the SDGs serve to bring clarity and focus to efforts to address critical issues on a global scale. In some ways, they have been highly effective: Organizations highlight the SDG goals they are addressing; funders channel resources toward specific goals; and the United Nations assesses progress against these goals annually. As intended, the goals serve to align the international community around a clear set of outcomes (UNDP, 2024).

In recent years, though, it has become clear that we are not making fast enough progress against these goals. We are not on a path to achieve these goals by 2030, and many in the international community have been wondering what could be done to accelerate that progress.

Around 2020, some of the most influential thought leaders from the fields of psychology, adult development, leadership and organizational development were consulted to explore this challenge. We're talking about people like Peter Senge, the guru of systems thinking, Otto Scharmer, the creator of Theory U, Amy Edmondson, the Harvard professor whose work focuses on psychological safety, and Bob Kegan, the Harvard professor who is one of the most influential scholars of adult development. These are some of the folks who were involved in this exploration of what might be done to move the needle more effectively on the SDGs. The concept of a set of Inner Development Goals (IDGs) emerged from those conversations (IDG, 2021, p. 5).

The essence of the idea was simple but profound: We must complement that outer-world focus of the SDGs with an equally intentional focus on the inner capacities that we individually and collectively need to cultivate to effectively create the impact we need to see in the world.

Once the idea of developing a set of IDGs was hatched, a collection of funders and academic institutions came together to form the IDG Foundation to move the ball forward. The Foundation launched a research initiative that included engaging more academic experts and crafting a survey that was completed by more than 800 researchers, practitioners, and experts from around the globe (IDG, 2021). From that process emerged the IDG framework as it currently stands. Here it is:

As you can see, the IDGs include five dimensions and 23 skills. The five dimensions are *Being, Thinking, Relating, Collaborating, and Acting* (Fig. 8). Each of these dimensions includes a subset of specific skills related to that dimension.

The similarities between this IDG framework and the Flame and Journey model that I've shared in this book are impossible to miss. At this highest level, the Being, Thinking, and Acting dimensions of the IDGs correlate closely with the Be, Know, and Do elements of the Flame. On a more detailed level, the specific skills listed in the IDGs are exactly the skills that are cultivated by the Flame and Journey model. For example, the "Being" dimension of the IDGs includes skills like "Inner Compass," "Integrity and Authenticity," and "Self Awareness." Exercises like the Mission and Shadow serve to develop exactly those skills. The "Thinking" dimension includes skills like "critical thinking," "complexity aware-ness," "perspective skills," and "sense-making." Again, these are exactly the skills that are cultivated by the Question Formulation Process and Journey reflection experiences.

I could go on, but a detailed analysis of how these two models overlap and how they differ is beyond the scope of this chapter. The point that I want to highlight here is the unmistakable degree of overlap between these two approaches to inner development. Although the two models were devel-oped in complete isolation, they illuminate a similar landscape of key concepts and important skills. As you've learned, the Flame and Journey model was refined through years of trial and error focused on finding ways to make inner development happen powerfully and at scale in organizations where I worked. The IDGs evolved through a different path of consultation with thought leaders, input from hundreds of practitioners, and rigorous engagement with relevant research and literature. Both paths converged on frameworks for

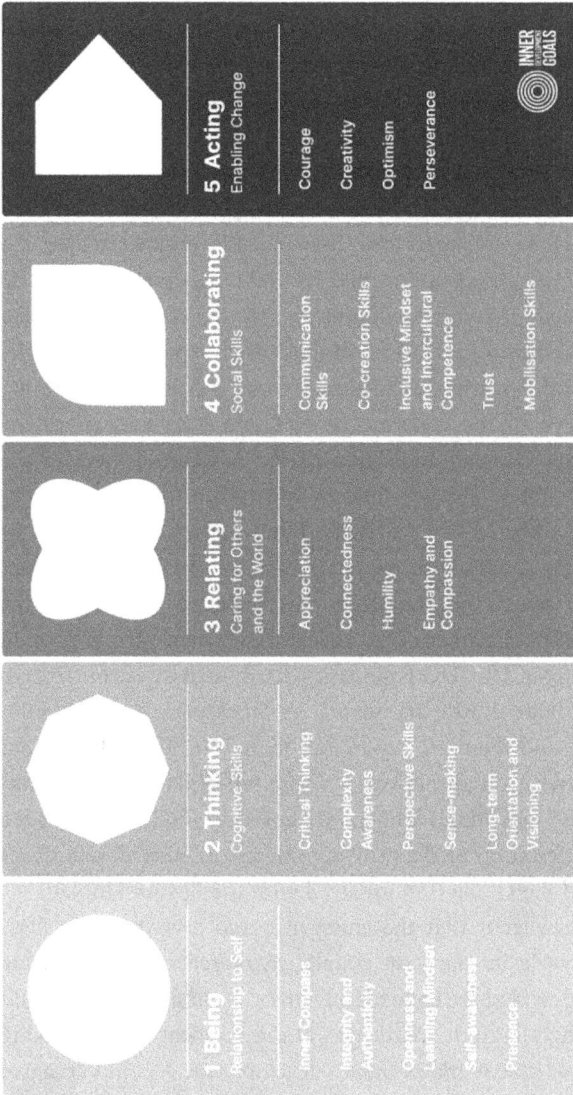

Fig. 8.   The IDG Framework: Source: Inner Development Goals, Framework.

understanding and engaging in inner development that are surprisingly similar.

I first learned about the IDG framework in 2022, after I had already spent decades developing the Flame and Journey approach described in this book. I was thrilled to discover an initiative highlighting the need to complement a rigorous focus on impact with an equally rigorous focus on inner development; this was the motivation behind everything I had been working on for years. It's been equally exciting to see the remarkable momentum that is building around the IDG movement. In just a couple years, the IDGs have been embraced by organizations in the business world, like Google, Ikea, and Novartis. In the public sector, it is already informing the work of the government of Costa Rica as well as the National Oceanic and Atmospheric Association here in the United States. The key funders and staff of the IDG foundation were invited to the White House in the Fall of 2024 to share the model with members of the Biden administration, and a session on the IDGs was included in COP29 (the international gathering to discuss environmental action) in Azerbaijan. The IDG Foundation has hosted three conferences with about 1,500 attendants in Stockholm and 10,000+ online, and there are now more than 750 "IDG Hubs" that are active around the world. These self-organized local gatherings of individuals who are enthusiastic about this work are a manifestation of the growing interest in inner development around the Globe (I'm involved with the Boston Hub).

My belief is that the emergence and growth of the IDG framework in the last couple years reflects the growing awareness that we have hit the limits of our ability to respond meaningfully to the challenges of this moment without taking seriously the work of inner development. I couldn't agree more that our critical focus on addressing pressing public challenges needs to be complemented with an equally rigorous focus on developing the inner capacities of those seeking to create change. I believe that the Flame and Journey work and the IDG framework are both manifestations of this emerging awareness that we need to take inner development seriously if we want to respond meaningfully to the challenges of our time. It is my fervent hope that the ideas presented in this book contribute powerfully to this growing movement to integrate a dual focus on outer and inner change in effective and scalable ways in the years ahead.

CLOSING THOUGHTS

In this book, I've sought to share all I've learned from years of experimenting with an approach to organizational development that clearly integrates the inner and outer dimensions of change. It's an approach that honors the well-known power of organizational culture to shape individual and collective performance. It also recognizes the need for clear roles and effective performance management efforts – all the work that relates to the "DO" and "KNOW" levels of the Flame. It complements all that organizational work with a new capacity to invite people to focus on the innermost "BE" level of the Flame in powerful and scalable ways.

I'll bring this book to a conclusion with my favorite Joseph Campbell quote. It was featured in the beginning of this book, and it highlights an insight that is central to the Flame and Journey approach described in these pages. In his book *Primitive Mythology*, Campbell says:

> *For we move – each – in two worlds: The inward of our own awareness and an outwards of participation in the history of our time and place (p. 92).*

There is a role for organizations to play in honoring this interconnection between our two worlds. I hope I have demonstrated here that it is possible for organizations to do this work powerfully and at scale. It is my deepest hope that this book might help more organizations embrace the work of integrating these interconnected and interdependent inner and outer worlds in the years ahead.

APPENDIX 1: CITY YEAR CORE VALUES

1. Service to a cause greater than self

We dedicate ourselves to addressing shared civic challenges through unified action.

City Year believes that service is a personal decision to dedicate one's time, energy, and effort to a cause greater than oneself. It's also a way to bring together diverse individuals who share a common goal while strengthening our country and our communities. At City Year, we make a collective effort to demonstrate the power of service as a way to connect us to the fullness of what democracy and citizenship should be – teaching us the shared responsibility we have to each other and showing us what can be achieved through collaboration and determination.

2. Students first, collaboration always

The success of the young people we serve is our preeminent goal, best achieved by working in partnership with others who are dedicated to the same cause.

We are fiercely committed to dedicating our resources and energy in an effort to positively impact the lives of our students and their families while supporting the success of our AmeriCorps members. We recognize that this goal can only be achieved by working together with others – teachers, administrators, parents, policymakers and partners – who share our commitment to creating environments that will help students build on their strengths and fully engage in their learning.

3. Belief in the power of young people

We are committed to harnessing one of the most powerful forces for positive change at work in the world today.

The energy and idealism of young people are two of the most powerful and transformative forces at work in the world today. From advancing social justice in the United States, to youth-led movements around the world, the dedication of young people is driving major change. At City Year, we're committed to tapping this power to help create more equitable access to education opportunities for students in systemically under-resourced schools. In the process, we're striving to help foster a generation of empowered, experienced, effective, and idealistic leaders. Because our experience has shown that young people surpass the highest of expectations to achieve extraordinary results.

4. Social justice for all

We dedicate ourselves to building a more just, equal, fair and compassionate world.

We recognize that unequal access to opportunity along lines of race, class, gender, sexual orientation, ability, age, and other aspects of identity has deep roots in our country – including in our education system and all the systems that we operate in – creating persistent and deep inequities. To work toward greater educational equity for all, we must deeply understand and enable the conditions to promote diversity, equity, inclusivity and belonging in our organization and in the communities we serve.

5. Level five leadership

We aspire to develop a culture of "level five leadership" across the organization, fostering a blend of great humility with intense professional will.

The concept of "level five leadership" is borrowed from the book *Good to Great*, written by Jim Collins. The term describes a style of leadership that blends a paradoxical mix of qualities. First, level five leaders practice great humility: they are modest, they learn from and listen to others, they give credit to others for success, and they take personal responsibility when things don't go as planned. At the same time, they work with intense professional will: they take bold action, set ambitious goals, make courageous decisions, and persevere through the long, challenging process of achieving great things. Humility, will, boldness, courage, and perseverance: these are the qualities of level five leadership, and City Year is committed to operating in this way across our organization.

6. Empathy

We strive to learn from the perspective and experiences of others.

City Year believes that empathy is an essential skill for anyone committed to social change. Given the complexity of the issues we seek to address and the diversity of our staff, AmeriCorps members, students, and communities, a strong capacity for empathy is essential. Empathy enables us to collaborate effectively, build trust, and deepen understanding, which consequently strengthens our program's design, implementation, and results.

7. Inclusivity

We embrace differences as strengths that magnify our capacity to achieve shared goals.

Inclusivity involves more than the celebration of diversity. It means actively embracing differences as vital assets that enrich our community, ensuring that people with different identities feel welcome, valued, empowered, and engaged. Inclusivity informs our strategy of engaging young people in our service, listening to students about how to create learning environments, and our commitment to partner across the public, private, and nonprofit sectors in order to drive systemic change.

8. Ubuntu

I am a person through other people; my humanity is tied to yours.

Ubuntu – a term borrowed from the Zulu tribe of South Africa – means "I am a person through other people; my humanity is tied to yours." This concept expresses a spiritual truth about the world: we're all connected to each other through invisible webs of interdependence. We share a common world and destiny, and the struggles of a few can affect the many. Because of this connection, we're able to deepen our own humanity when we're able to recognize and honor the humanity of those around us. This belief informs our commitment to treating everyone we interact with deep respect. It's simply a way of being and a quality of presence that we aspire to bring into all of our relationships.

9. Teamwork

We strive to work powerfully together in a unified effort to achieve our goals.

At City Year, we believe deeply in the power of teams. When a group of diverse individuals unite, collaborate, and dream together in pursuit of a shared goal, the team becomes more powerful than the sum of its parts. In the words of Margaret

Mead, "Never doubt that a small group of thoughtful, committed citizens can change the world. Indeed, it's the only thing that ever has." That's why City Year has made teamwork essential to every single thing we do. From AmeriCorps members who are working together every day to support student success, to staff members at all levels who work collaboratively to advance our organizational goals and mission, everyone at City Year operates as part of a team. And as a result, our teamwork continually helps us maximize our impact and engenders respect, empathy, understanding, communication, insight, patience, creativity, and joy.

10. Excellence

We hold ourselves to the highest standards as we strive to execute our mission and steward our resources.

City Year recognizes that our goals for change can only be achieved through disciplined, rigorous, and tireless attention to detail. Excellence is both an inspiring vision and a daily practice. It informs the goals that we set for ourselves, as well as the dedication we put forward to achieve those goals. We know that the smallest details influence the grandest of outcomes, which is why we aspire to achieve excellence not only in the execution of our mission but also in the way we manage our resources.

This list is viewable at https://www.cityyear.org/about/values/

REFERENCES

Bar-Yam, Y. (1992). *Dynamics of complex systems*. Perseus Books.

Beck, J. (2019, December 11). This article won't change your mind: The facts on why facts can't fight false beliefs. *The Atlantic*. https://www.theatlantic.com/science/archive/2017/03/this-article-wont-change-your-mind/519093/. Accessed on December 20, 2024.

Beck, D. E., & Cowan, C. C. (2006). *Spiral dynamics: Mastering values, leadership, and change*. Blackwell Publishing.

Bierut, M. (2012). *79 short essays on design*. Princeton Architectural Press.

Brooks, D. (2011). *The social animal: The hidden sources of love, character, and achievement*. Random House.

Buckingham, M., & Goodall, A. (2015, April). Reinventing performance management. *Harvard Business Review*. https://hbr.org/2015/04/reinventing-performance-management

Campbell, J. (1949). *The hero with a thousand faces*. MJF Books.

Campbell, J. (1988). *The power of myth*. Anchor Books.

Campbell, J. (1991). *The masks of god: Creative mythology*. Penguin Arkana Books.

Campbell, J. (2004). *Pathways to bliss: Mythology and personal transformation*. New World Library.

Campbell, J., Moyers, B., & Cousineau, P. (1990). *The hero's journey: Joseph Campbell on his life and work* (P. Cousineau, Ed.). New World Library.

Catmull, E. (2014). *Creativity, Inc.: Overcoming the unseen forces that stand in the way of true inspiration.* Random House.

Center for Creative Leadership. (2020, November 4). *The 70-20-10 rule for leadership development.* Center for Creative Leadership. https://www.ccl.org/articles/leading-effectively-articles/70-20-10-rule/. Accessed on May, 2021.

Cole, D. (2002). *Immigrant city: Lawrence, Massachusetts, 1845–1921.* The University of North Carolina Press.

Collins, T. (1997). *Mythic Reflections: Thoughts on myth, spirit, and our times.* Context Institute. https://www.context.org/iclib/ic12/campbell. Accessed on May, 2021.

Collins, J., & Porras, J. (1994). *Built to last: Successful habits of visionary companies.* Harper Business.

Dutton, J. E., & Wrzesniewski, A. (2020, March 12). What job crafting looks like. *Harvard Business Review.* https://hbr.org/2020/03/what-job-crafting-looks-like

Franklin, B. (1758). *Poor richards almanac.* https://archive.org/details/poorrichardsalma00franrich/page/56/mode/2up. Accessed on December 20, 2024.

Greenleaf, R. (2002). *Servant leadership: A journey into the nature of legitimate power and greatness.* Paulist Press.

Hastings, R., & Meyer, E. (2020). *No rules rules: Netflix and the culture of reinvention.* Penguin Press.

Heifetz, R. (1994). *Leadership without easy answers.* Harvard University Press.

Heifetz, R., Linksy, M., & Grashow, A. (2009). *The practice of adaptive leadership: Tools and tactics for changing your organization and the world*. Harvard Business Press.

Heifetz, R., & Linsky, M. (2017). *Leadership on the line*. Harvard Business Review Press.

Inner Development Goals. (2021). *Inner development goals: Background, method and the IDG framework*. Inner Development Goals. https://innerdevelopmentgoals.org/about/resources/

Inner Development Goals. (2024). *Framework*. https://innerdevelopmentgoals.org/framework/

Jobs, S. (1998, May 25). *There is sanity returning*. Business Week.

Jung, C. (1933). *Modern man in search of a soul*. Harcourt, Brace & World, Inc.

Jung, C. (1968). *Psychology and alchemy*. Princeton University Press.

Jung, C. (1976). *The portable jung* (J. Cambpell, Ed.). Penguin Books.

Jung, C. (1981). *The archetypes and the collective unconscious*. Princeton University Press.

Kegan, R., & Lahey, L. (2016). *An everyone culture: Becoming a deliberately development organization*. Harvard Business Review Press.

Kellerman, B. (2014). *Hard times: Leadership in America*. Stanford Business Books.

Kennedy, R. (1966, June 6). *Day of affirmation address.*
University of Cape Town. https://www.jfklibrary.org/learn/
about-jfk/the-kennedy-family/robert-f-kennedy/robert-f-
kennedy-speeches/day-of-affirmation-address-university-of-
capetown-capetown-south-africa-june-6-1966

Klau, M. (2017). *Race and social change: A quest, A study, A
call to action.* Jossey Bass.

Laloux, F. (2014). *Reinventing organizations: A guide to
creating organizations inspired by the next stage in human
consciousness.* Nelson Parker.

Laloux, F. (2015, July 6). *Strategy+Business.* https://www.
strategy-business.com/article/00344?gko=30876

Lasse, C. (2015, November 20). *What is a competency?*
Association for Talent Develoment. https://www.td.org/
insights/what-is-a-competency

MacWilliams, M. (2016, January 17). *Politico Magazine.*
Politico. https://www.politico.com/magazine/story/2016/01/
donald-trump-2016-authoritarian-213533/

Meredith, J., & Anderson, L. M. (2015). *Analysis of the
impacts of city year's whole school whole child model on
partner school's performance.* Policy Studies Associates.

Petrie, N. (2011). *Future trends in leadership development.*
Center for Creative Leadership.

Pfeffer, J. (2015). *Leadership BS: Fixing workplaces and
careers one truth at a time.* Harper Business.

Robinson, W. V. (2014, October 17). Seth moulton
underplays military service. *Boston Globe.* https://www.
bostonglobe.com/metro/2014/10/17/moulton-underplays-
military-service/lY9FfmOrviwL2LAFHr61dO/story.html

Roosevelt, T. (1910, April 23). *"Citizenship in a republic"
speech*. https://www.theodorerooseveltcenter.org/Learn-
About-TR/TR-Encyclopedia/Culture-and-Society/Man-in-the-
Arena.aspx. Accessed on December 20, 2024

Rothstein, D., & Santana, L. (2011). *Make just one change:
Teach students to ask their own questions*. Harvard Education
Press.

Rothstein, D., Santana, L., & Bain, A. (2016). *Partnering with
parents to ask the right questions: A powerful strategy for
strengthening school-family partnerships*. ASCD.

Scharmer, C. O. (2003). *The blind spot of leadership:
Presencing as a social technology of freedom*. https://
bhavanalearninggroup.com/wp-content/uploads/2014/08/
2003_TheBlindSpot.pdf

Schein, E. H. (1985). *Organizational culture and leadership*.
Jossey-Bass.

Scullen, S., Mount, M., & Goff, M. (2000). Understanding the
Latent Structure of job performance ratings. *Journal of
Applied Psychology*, *85*(6), 956–970.

Solzhenitsyn, A. (2007). *The gulag archipelago, volume 1*.
Harper Perennial Modern Classics.

The Right Question Institute. (2021). *Microdemocracy*. Right
Question Institute. https://rightquestion.org/microdemocracy/.
Accessed on May, 2021.

United Nations Development Programme. (2024). *Sustainable
development goals: Background on the goals*. https://www.
undp.org/sdg-accelerator/background-goals

Wheatley, M. (2006). *Leadership and the new science:
Discovering order in a chaotic world*. Berret-Koehler.

Wheatley, M., & Frieze, D. (2010, Winter). *Leadership in the age of complexity: From hero to host.* margaretwheatley.com. https://www.margaretwheatley.com/articles/Leadership-in-Age-of-Complexity.pdf

Wrzesniewski, A., & Dutton, J. (2001, April). Crafting a job: Revisioning employees as active crafters of their work. *Academy of Management Review*, 26(2), 179–201.

INDEX